Published in 2022 by Are Media Books, Australia.
Are Media Books is a division of Are Media Pty Ltd.

ARE MEDIA

Chief executive officer
Jane Huxley

ARE MEDIA BOOKS

Group publisher
Nicole Byers

Editorial & food director
Sophia Young

Books director
David Scotto

Creative director
Hannah Blackmore

Managing editor
Stephanie Kistner

Senior designer
Kelsie Walker

Editor
Amanda Lees

Food editors
Amanda Chebatte,
Domenica Reddie

**BDM Custom Publishing
& International Rights**
Amanda Atkinson
amanda.atkinson@aremedia.com.au

Photographers
James Moffatt, Luisa Brimble

Stylist
Olivia Blackmore

Photochef
Clare Maguire

Printed in China by
1010 Printing International

A catalogue record for this book
is available from the National
Library of Australia.
ISBN 978-1-92586-683-4

© Are Media Pty Limited 2022
ABN 18 053 273 546

Published by Are Media Books,
a division of Are Media Pty Limited,
54 Park St, Sydney; GPO Box 4088,
Sydney, NSW 2001, Australia
Ph +61 2 9282 8000;
www.awwcookbooks.com.au

International rights enquiries
internationalrights@aremedia.com.au

Order books
phone 1300 322 007 (within Australia)

or order online at
www.awwcookbooks.com.au

Send recipe enquiries to
recipeenquiries@aremedia.com.au

The publisher would like to thank
Barbeques Galore for providing the
barbecues used in this book.

barbequesgalore.com.au

 womensweeklyfood

 @womensweeklyfood

 TRUSTED BRANDS USED IN OUR TEST KITCHEN

THE AUSTRALIAN
Women's Weekly

FIRE
GRILL
SMOKE

THE AUSTRALIAN WOMEN'S WEEKLY TEST KITCHEN
TEST KITCHEN TESTED

CONTENTS

ABOUT BARBECUING

The backyard barbecue has come a long way from the days of chargrilling some sausages. Now it's an indispensable part of summer life – and with instant gas and electric barbecues, some people barbecue every single night. When choosing a barbecue, consider the amount of space you have and the type of fuel you would prefer to use.

BARBECUES

Trolley barbecues with wheels, are essentially portable, but are usually set up as a permanent or semi-permanent unit. Most modern trolley barbecues use gas and most are fitted with hoods, allowing for covered and uncovered cooking.

Kettle barbecues such as the Weber, have domed lids and are meant to be used for covered cooking, although they can be used for quick, uncovered grilling. They usually have temperature gauges and are portable.

Open barbecues which are the barbecues you generally see at the park or picnic areas, do not have hoods and are used solely for direct cooking and grilling. They are generally one large flat cooking plate, made from cast iron or stainless steel. They can be a permanent fixture or portable.

Hibachi barbecues are portable, small, open (no hood), cast iron barbecues which are perfect for camping, a picnic or the beach. They are just large enough to cook food for two or three people. A grill or metal flat plate, supported on bricks over an open fire can be used the same way.

SMOKING

This is a cooking style in which the flavours of the food are affected by the choice of wood used. Soaked wood chips and herbs are placed in a smoke box, allowing the items to combust slowly without causing flare-ups. During preheating, place the smoke box over the heat source. When smoke appears from within the box, adjust the burners on a gas barbecue to low. If using a charcoal barbecue, place the smoke box directly under the food and use indirect heat. For best results, try not to interrupt cooking by frequently opening the lid.

DIY BARBECUE SMOKER BOX

You can use a smoker box to hold the wood chips and follow the instructions for your barbecue, or substitute with a disposable foil pie tin. Add the food to be smoked once the chips start to smoke, either directly on the grill plate or in a separate container, then cook with the lid closed. For charcoal barbecues, lumps of smoking wood are added directly to the coals.

TOP TIPS FOR BARBECUE SMOKING

- Don't overdo the wood chips – it creates too much smoke and makes the food taste bitter.

- The smoke should gently waft, not billow out.

- Aim for white or blue smoke, not black – black smoke indicates insufficient ventilation or that the food is too close to the heat and the juices are burning, which can taint the flavour of the meat.

- Keep air circulating – keep the vents of the lid open, so the smoke swirls around the food.

MEAT THERMOMETER

Invest in a meat thermometer, as this ensures the meat reaches the correct temperature to be cooked by the smoking process.

CLEANING

All barbecues should be cleaned after cooking; close hood on the barbecue, turn the setting to the highest possible heat, and let any food residue burn off. Turn the barbecue off and use a metal scraper to loosen any remaining food residue, picking them up or wiping them off as you go. As soon as possible after barbecuing, with heat turned off, and while the barbecue is still hot, clean all cooking surfaces with a wire brush dipped in water (not soapy). Wipe dry with newspaper. When cool and completely dry, spray or brush lightly with canola oil (to prevent rust), wipe off the surplus before covering the barbecue with a vinyl cover for weather protection.

USEFUL TIPS

Preheating barbecue Use the highest setting with hood closed, until barbecue reaches the desired temperature. For direct cooking, heat barbecue for about 6–7 minutes (or longer if using wood, heat beads or coal) and for indirect cooking, heat for about 3–4 minutes (or follow the manufacturer's instructions).

Heat test Make sure the barbecue is at the temperature required for the recipe before adding the food. A good heat test is to see how long you can hold your hand just above the surface of the grill. It is a very hot fire if you can hold your hand in place for one second or less, three seconds for a medium-hot barbecue, and five seconds for a low-medium fire.

Cooking oil spray Never spray a barbecue with cooking oil while switched on; if the oil hits the flame or heat source it may cause a dangerous flare-up.

Barbecue safety Always keep a spray bottle filled with water to douse flare-ups. It will not affect the food being cooked on gas barbecues but will cause ash to rise and settle on the food when cooking with wood or charcoal, so only use as a last resort.

Sausages Don't prick sausages as this allows the moisture to leak out, leaving them dry and tasteless. Sausages should take a long time to cook over a low heat; if they look like they are about to burst, move them to a cooler part of the barbecue.

FIRE

CHARCOAL INFUSES YOUR FOOD WITH A FLAVOUR
THAT YOUR GAS BARBECUE JUST CAN'T REPLICATE.
IT'S A SUBTLE SMOKY PRESENCE THAT TRANSFORMS
YOUR STEAK, FISH OR VEG FROM THE ORDINARY INTO
SOMETHING COMPLEX AND ABSOLUTELY DELICIOUS.

HOW TO GET YOUR CHARCOAL FIRE GOING

BUY GOOD-QUALITY CHARCOAL

Always try and buy good-quality sustainably produced charcoal – look at your supermarket or barbecue stores for charcoal made from coppiced wood or Forestry Commission-approved wood. This charcoal lights easily, burns better and won't taint the flavour of the food, unlike charcoals containing accelerants.

USE A CHARCOAL CHIMNEY OR STACK

A charcoal chimney is a metal cylinder with a grate at the bottom, holes in the side, and a handle on the side which means you can light charcoal easily with a few sheets of newspaper – the coals will catch and start glowing quickly and easily. A chimney also protects the coals (and you) on a windy day. Once the coals are ready, you can safely and easily tip them into the barbecue.

If you don't have a chimney, arrange your charcoal in a stack in barbecue or pit. Then push balls of newspaper or natural firelighters (such as wood shavings) between the charcoals. Light the paper and firelighters, and allow the flames to catch and get going in their own time. Then, let them die down again – all you're going to achieve with flames is burnt food. You need ashen coals to cook on.

When a few coals have been lit, the rest will catch on their own, so don't hurry them along by adding more firelighters. If the heat is starting to die down as you barbecue, add coals to the outside of the barbecue and leave them to flame up and die down before cooking over them.

How you arrange your coals will give you different heat zones and more control over your barbecue.

DIRECT HEAT

Barbecuing directly on heated up coals If you think of a barbecue as a stovetop, lighting an even layer of coal is the equivalent of cooking everything on the highest heat. Although this might be fine for thin cuts of meat that cook quickly, it will cremate anything that needs more time to cook through.

INDIRECT HEAT

Barbecuing on half heated up coals Push the coals to one side of the barbecue and keep the other side free to get a range of temperatures – use the coal-free side to cook by indirect heat. Hot coals on just one side also will enable you to cook on one half and keep food warm on the other.

Barbecuing with coals arranged with circular gap in the middle Sit an old roasting tray in the middle of the barbecue and stack the coals around it, then cook the food on the grill over the tray, again covered by the lid. The heat circulates around the barbecue giving you a hot smoker/spit-roast effect.

Cooking indirectly means food won't burn or scorch. It is perfect for larger joints and meat on the bone, such as chickens and lamb. It's also great for more delicate items, such as fish fillets. Plus it gives some direct heat where the coals are stacked should you want to brown other items quickly.

A LITTLE OF EACH – DIRECT AND INDIRECT HEAT

By sloping the coals you get a gradient of heat from searing hot to sizzling gently. This is useful when barbecuing for a crowd – you can keep things ticking over on one side while cooking at full heat on the other.

ASHY WHITE BUT STILL VERY HOT
Ready for indirect heat or cooking in the coals.

LEARN TO RECOGNISE WHEN YOUR COALS ARE READY

If you try to cook something when the coals aren't ready, it may overcook or burn – it's not a risk worth taking. Use our colour code guide to help decide when to start cooking your food.

BLACK OR GREY WITH FLAMES
Not ready yet. Step away, have a beer and relax.

GLOWING WHITE HOT WITH RED CENTRES
Ready for direct heat (blow gently on coals to check).

SERVES 4

PREP + COOK TIME 35 MINUTES (+ STANDING & HEATING)

GRILLED KING PRAWNS WITH MANDARIN OIL

_____

2 medium mandarins (400g)

2 tbsp coriander seeds

½ cup (125ml) grapeseed oil

1 tbsp smoked paprika

pinch of salt

1 tsp white wine vinegar

8 extra-large king prawns
  (800g), heads removed,
  butterflied with shell intact

Finely grate rind of mandarins, using a Microplane grater, if available; you will need 2 teaspoons rind. Juice mandarins; you will need ½ cup (125ml) juice.

To make mandarin oil, place coriander seeds in a small frying pan; toast, stirring over medium heat for 2 minutes or until fragrant. Add oil, paprika, salt and grated mandarin rind to pan. Gently heat for 5 minutes or until tiny bubbles begin to appear around the edge. Set aside, covered, for 1 hour to infuse. Strain before using.

Meanwhile, prepare a charcoal barbecue to medium heat according to instructions on pages 10-11.

Combine ¼ cup (60ml) of the mandarin juice with ¼ cup (60ml) of the mandarin oil. Reserve for serving.

Stir vinegar into remaining mandarin oil. Lightly brush flesh of prawns with oil mixture. Place prawns on grill, shell-side down. Cook for 5 minutes or until flesh is tender and cooked through. Remove from grill.

Serve prawns drizzled with reserved mandarin oil mixture.

TIP When barbecuing prawns (and other shellfish), it is always best to cook them shell-side down as it will gently cook the flesh. Turning them over results in them losing their natural juices. To butterfly prawns, run a knife, along the soft underbelly of each prawn, from head to tail without cutting all the way through.

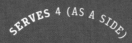

SERVES 4 (AS A SIDE)

PREP + COOK TIME 35 MINUTES (+ HEATING)

CHARRED SUGARLOAF CABBAGE WITH LEMON PARMESAN DRESSING

---

extra virgin olive oil,
for shallow-frying

¼ cup (50g) baby capers

2 large sugarloaf cabbages
(1kg), quartered lengthways

extra virgin olive oil, extra,
to drizzle

LEMON PARMESAN DRESSING

8 anchovy fillets, chopped finely

1 cup (80g) finely grated
parmesan, plus extra to serve

2 tbsp finely grated pecorino

2 tbsp finely chopped tarragon

1 tbsp lemon juice

⅔ cup (160ml) extra virgin
olive oil

Prepare a charcoal barbecue with hood to high heat according to instructions on pages 10-11.

Place enough oil in a small saucepan to come 2cm (¾in) up the side. Set pan over high heat. Pat capers dry with paper towel. Fry capers in hot oil for 2 minutes or until crisp. Remove capers using a slotted spoon; drain on paper towel.

Drizzle cabbage all over with extra oil; season. Cook cabbage on grill, turning frequently, for 15 minutes or until charred and tender-crisp.

Meanwhile, make lemon parmesan dressing.

Place cabbage in shallow bowls. Top with dressing, then scatter with crisp capers and extra parmesan.

LEMON PARMESAN DRESSING Place ingredients in a high speed blender. Blend until very well combined. Season to taste.

TIP If sugarloaf cabbage is unavailable, substitute with savoy, green, wombok or red cabbage, or even cos (romaine) or iceberg lettuce. The lettuce will require a shorter cooking time.

SERVES *8*

PREP + COOK TIME 50 MINUTES (+ OVERNIGHT REFRIGERATION & STANDING)

CITRUS-MARINATED LAMB GYROS

¼ cup dried Greek oregano

2 tbsp lemon rind

⅓ cup (80ml) lemon juice

2 tbsp orange rind

⅔ cup (160ml) orange juice

¾ cup (180ml) extra virgin olive oil

1kg (2lb) lamb leg, boned, butterflied

4 desiree potatoes (680g), scrubbed

2 x 220g (7oz) tubs store-bought tzatziki

2 tbsp finely chopped dill

8 Greek pitta

3 baby gem lettuce, leaves separated

1 small red onion (100g), sliced into rounds

You will need to start this recipe 1 day ahead.

Combine oregano, lemon rind and juice, orange rind and juice, and half the oil in a large bowl. Season. Add lamb and turn to coat well. Refrigerate, covered, overnight. Remove from fridge 1 hour before cooking to come to room temperature.

Meanwhile, prepare a charcoal barbecue to medium heat according to instructions on pages 10-11.

Cut potatoes into 1cm (½in) thick wedges; transfer to a medium bowl. Pour over enough boiling water to cover. Stand for 30 minutes. Drain potatoes; toss with remaining oil. Season.

Remove lamb from marinade; discard marinade. Cook lamb on grill for 20 minutes, turning halfway through cooking until charred on the outside and cooked to medium in the centre. Remove lamb from grill, transfer to a plate. Rest, loosely covered, for 10 minutes.

Meanwhile, cook potatoes on grill for 4 minutes each side or until charred and tender.

Combine dill and tzatziki in a small bowl.

Place pitta on grill; cook for 1 minute, turning halfway, until lightly charred and warmed through. Thinly slice lamb.

To assemble, top pitta with lettuce, lamb, potato wedges, tzatziki and onion. Serve immediately.

RECIPE PAGES 20-21

BUTTERFLIED SPATCHCOCK WITH SMOKED CHILLI AÏOLI

SERVES 4

PREP + COOK TIME 1 HOUR 15 MINUTES (+ OVERNIGHT REFRIGERATION, HEATING & RESTING)

BUTTERFLIED SPATCHCOCK WITH SMOKED CHILLI AÏOLI

————————

A SPATCHCOCK IS A SMALL CHICKEN, SOMETIMES
CALLED A POUSSIN, WHICH IS NO MORE THAN
6 WEEKS OLD AND WEIGHS A MAXIMUM OF 500G (1LB).
THEY ARE PERFECT FOR AN INDIVIDUAL PORTION,
MAKING A DECADENT BARBECUE CHICKEN DINNER.

YOU WILL NEED TO START THIS RECIPE 1 DAY AHEAD.

1kg (2lb) rock salt

2¼ cups (495g) brown sugar

1 tbsp lemon rind

2 tsp lime rind

5 cloves garlic, sliced thinly

½ bunch thyme, plus extra
   sprigs, to serve

½ bunch oregano

1½ tsp each fennel, coriander
   and cumin seeds, toasted

4 x 500g (1lb) spatchcock,
   butterflied (see tips)

2 tbsp extra virgin olive oil,
   plus extra to serve

lime halves, to serve

SMOKED CHILLI AÏOLI

5 fresh long red chillies

4 cloves garlic, crushed

300g (9½oz) Kewpie
   (Japanese) mayonnaise

2 tsp finely grated lemon rind

1 tbsp lemon juice

Process salt, sugar, lemon and lime rinds, garlic, herbs and seeds until just combined. Spread one-third of the mixture over the base of a large, non-reactive deep container. Pat spatchcocks dry with paper towel; sit spatchcocks in salt mixture and cover with remaining mixture. Cover container and refrigerate for 6 hours.

Remove spatchcocks, rinse off any salt mixture and pat dry with paper towel. Transfer to a wire rack set over a large tray. Refrigerate, uncovered, for 6 hours or overnight for skin to dry out.

Prepare a charcoal barbecue with hood to high heat according to instructions on pages 10-11.

Make smoked chilli aïoli.

Drizzle spatchcock with oil; thread evenly onto two large double pronged skewers. Cook, skin-side down on the barbecue grill, turning frequently for 40 minutes or until cooked through and skin is charred (see tips). Remove; loosely cover with foil. Stand for 10 minutes.

Meanwhile, grill lime halves, cut-side down, for 1 minute or until charred and grill marks appear.

Drizzle spatchcock with extra oil. Season. Serve with aïoli and lime halves.

SMOKED CHILLI AÏOLI
Pierce chillies with the tip of a sharp knife then place directly on hot coals. Cook, turning occasionally, for 10 minutes or until blackened and blistered. Transfer to a heatproof bowl and cover; stand for 15 minutes. Peel away charred skin and remove seeds and stalks; discard. Leave to cool. Combine chillies, garlic, mayonnaise, lemon rind and juice in a high speed blender or a small food processor. Blend until smooth. Season to taste.

TIPS Ask the butcher to butterfly the spatchcocks for you. When barbecuing, ensure the coals are very hot but without flames. Cooking over a flame will burn the outside before the flesh is cooked through. Spatchcocks are cooked when they reach an internal temperature of 75°C/170°F on a meat thermometer.

SERVES 4-6
(AS A STARTER)

PREP + COOK TIME 30 MINUTES (+ HEATING)

CHARRED FETTA WRAPPED IN VINE LEAVES

1 tbsp za'atar

3 tsp finely grated lemon rind

¼ cup (60ml) extra virgin olive oil

8 grape vine leaves, rinsed, patted dry (see Glossary, page 181)

2 x 200g (6½oz) blocks Greek fetta

1 tbsp honey

extra honey, thyme leaves and sesame lavosh, to serve

Prepare a charcoal barbecue with hood to high heat according to instructions on pages 10-11.

Combine za'atar, lemon rind and oil in a small bowl.

Lay 4 grape vine leaves in a round shape with leaves overlapping and no gaps. Place a block of fetta in the centre. Spoon over half the za'atar mixture, brushing to coat fetta all over. Drizzle with half the honey. Fold leaves over fetta to enclose and create a little parcel. Repeat with remaining vine leaves, fetta, za'atar mixture and honey.

Place fetta parcels on grill; close hood. Cook for 10 minutes, turning regularly. Open hood, cook for a further 5 minutes, turning occasionally or until vine leaves are charred and cheese is warm and soft all the way through.

Serve fetta parcels straight away, with extra honey, thyme and sesame lavosh.

TIP You can also cook the fetta parcels on a gas barbecue.

SERVES 6

PREP + COOK TIME 20 MINUTES (+ HEATING)

NEW ORLEANS– STYLE BBQ OYSTERS

———

70g (2½oz) unsalted butter

1 clove garlic, crushed

2 dozen shucked oysters

40g (1½oz) very finely grated parmesan (see tips)

2 tbsp finely chopped flat-leaf parsley

Tabasco, to taste

Prepare a charcoal barbecue to high heat according to instructions on pages 10-11.

Heat butter and garlic in a small saucepan over over hot coals. Cook for 5 minutes or until butter is bubbling. Remove from heat. Stand for 10 minutes.

Place oysters on grill. Evenly spoon garlic butter into shells. Sprinkle with parmesan and parsley. Cook for 3 minutes or until butter is bubbling and parmesan begins to melt.

Serve immediately with Tabasco.

TIPS Use the smallest holes on your box grater or a Microplane to grate the parmesan – it should resemble the texture of almond meal. Handle oysters gently as shells will be quite hot – oyster forks will help.

SERVES *4*

PREP + COOK TIME 15 MINUTES (+ HEATING & STANDING)

T–BONE STEAKS WITH TAHINI BBQ SAUCE

2 x 450g (14½oz) T-bone steaks

1 tbsp extra virgin olive oil

TAHINI BBQ SAUCE
¾ cup (180ml) tahini
2 cloves garlic, crushed
1 tsp chipotle chilli powder
2 tbsp pomegranate molasses

Prepare a charcoal barbecue to high heat according to instructions on pages 10-11. Sit grill 20cm (8in) above glowing coals.

Make tahini BBQ sauce.

Stand steaks at room temperature for 20 minutes. Brush with oil. Season.

Cook steaks on grill for 3 minutes each side. Brush with some of the tahini BBQ sauce; cook for a further 3 minutes, turning, for medium-rare, or until cooked to your liking. Remove. Cover; rest for 10 minutes.

Serve steaks with remaining tahini BBQ sauce.

TAHINI BBQ SAUCE Place ingredients with ½ cup (125ml) water in a small bowl; stir until smooth. (Makes 1½ cups.)

SERVES 6

PREP + COOK TIME 2 HOURS 10 MINUTES (+ COOLING & HEATING)

GRILLED OCTOPUS WITH MACADAMIA AJO BLANCO

---

2 x 1kg (2lb) tenderised octopus, cleaned

2¼ cups (560ml) extra virgin olive oil

2 cups (500ml) dry white wine

1 garlic bulb, halved horizontally

6 thyme sprigs

3 bay leaves

1 tbsp fennel seeds

2 lemons (280g), rind peeled thinly

1kg (2lb) kipfler potatoes, scrubbed, halved lengthways

¼ cup (40g) caperberries, drained

chilli oil, to serve

MACADAMIA AJO BLANCO

⅔ cup (90g) roasted macadamias, plus extra, chopped, to serve

50g (1½oz) stale sourdough bread, torn

2 tbsp extra virgin olive oil

1 tbsp sherry vinegar

Cut octopus into individual tentacles, trimming excess skin. Place 2 cups (500ml) of the olive oil, the wine, garlic, thyme, bay leaves, fennel seeds, lemon rind and 2 cups (500ml) water in a large saucepan over medium-high heat. Bring to a gentle simmer. Reduce heat to low. Add octopus. Cook, covered, for 1½ hours or until very tender. Remove. Cool completely in pan with lid on. Remove octopus from braising liquid; reserve.

Prepare a charcoal barbecue to medium heat according to instructions on pages 10-11. Temperature should read about 200°C/400°F on a thermometer.

Meanwhile, make macadamia ajo blanco.

Coat potatoes in half the remaining oil; season. Cook potatoes on grill, turning occasionally, for 15 minutes or until golden. Remove from grill; cover to keep warm.

Coat octopus in remaining oil. Cook octopus on grill for 4 minutes each side or until just charred.

Spoon ajo blanco onto serving plates. Top with octopus, extra macadamias and caperberries. Drizzle with chilli oil.

MACADAMIA AJO BLANCO Place macadamias and bread in a small bowl; cover with 1 cup (250ml) boiling water and stand for 15 minutes to soften. Place soaked macadamia and bread mixture with remaining ingredients in a high-speed blender. Blend until very smooth. Season to taste. Cover and set aside at room temperature until ready to serve.

TIP Macadamia ajo blanco can be refrigerated, covered, for up to 1 week.

SERVES 4

PREP + COOK TIME 1 HOUR (+ REFRIGERATION & HEATING)

YAKITORI CHICKEN AND BLISTERED EDAMAME

_____

500g (1lb) chicken thigh fillets, cut into 3cm (1¼in) pieces

6 green onions (scallions), trimmed, cut into 4cm (1½in) lengths

1½ cups (300g) brown rice

1 tbsp sesame oil

2⅔ cups (400g) frozen edamame pods

2 medium avocados (500g), cut into wedges

¼ cup (70g) pickled ginger

5g (¼oz) snack pack roasted nori (seaweed), snipped into thin strips with scissors

2 tsp each black and white sesame seeds, toasted

YAKITORI SAUCE

¼ cup (60ml) mirin

½ cup (125ml) soy sauce

2 tbsp rice wine vinegar

2 tbsp caster (superfine) sugar

4cm (1½in) ginger, sliced thinly

Make yakitori sauce.

Thread chicken and green onion onto 8 small wooden skewers, alternating pieces. Thread remaining green onion onto another 2 small wooden skewers. Brush chicken skewers with ¼ cup yakitori sauce. Refrigerate for 1 hour to marinate.

Meanwhile, prepare a charcoal barbecue or hibachi to high heat according to instructions on pages 10-11.

Place rice and 800ml water in a medium saucepan over medium heat on the stove. Bring to the boil; cook, uncovered, for 25 minutes or until rice is tender. Drain. Set aside to cool.

Brush chicken and green onion skewers with sesame oil. Cook skewers on grill, turning frequently, for 6 minutes or until charred and chicken is cooked through, occasionally brushing with some of the remaining marinade. Cook green onion skewers, for 3 minutes, turning frequently or until lightly charred.

Cook edamame on grill, turning, for 4 minutes or until charred.

Divide rice among bowls. Top with skewers and edamame. Serve with avocado, pickled ginger and nori. Drizzle with remaining yakitori sauce. Sprinkle with sesame seeds.

YAKITORI SAUCE Combine ingredients in a small saucepan over medium heat on the stove. Bring to a simmer, cook for 3 minutes or until reduced by half. Set aside to cool. (Makes ¾ cup.)

MAKES *4*

PREP + COOK TIME 30 MINUTES (+ STANDING & HEATING)

CHARRED SPANAKOPITA STUFFED FLATBREADS

⅔ cup (70g) grated mozzarella

150g (4½oz) firm fetta, crumbled

¼ cup chopped dill

2 tbsp finely chopped oregano

2¼ cups (90g) firmly packed baby spinach leaves, chopped

DOUGH

2 tsp (7g) dried yeast

1 tsp caster (superfine) sugar

½ cup (125ml) warm milk

2½ cups (375g) bread flour

½ tsp salt

LEMON SALSA

1 small lemon (65g)

1 tbsp chopped dill

1 green onion (scallion), chopped finely

2 tbsp pine nuts, toasted, chopped coarsely

1 tbsp extra virgin olive oil

Make dough.

Prepare a charcoal barbecue with hood to high heat according to instructions on pages 10-11.

Combine mozzarella, fetta, dill, oregano and spinach in a large bowl. Season.

Turn dough out onto a lightly floured surface. Divide dough into 8 portions. Roll each portion into a 12cm (4¾in) round. Divide cheese mixture between half the rounds, spooning mixture into the centre, leaving a 1cm (½in) border. Brush edges with water and top with remaining dough rounds, pressing edges to seal. Brush with oil; season.

Place flatbreads on grill. Cover with hood. Cook for 4 minutes. Turn flatbreads over; cook, covered, for a further 4 minutes or until bread is charred and cooked through.

Meanwhile, make lemon salsa.

Serve flatbread cut in half, with lemon salsa.

DOUGH Combine yeast, sugar, milk and ½ cup (125ml) water in a small bowl; stand for 5 minutes or until mixture is bubbly on the surface. Place flour and salt in a large bowl of an electric mixer with dough hook attached. On low speed, gradually add yeast mixture, until combined. Increase speed to high; mix for 6 minutes or until smooth and elastic. Transfer to a large lightly oiled bowl. Cover with a damp tea towel. Stand for 40 minutes or until doubled in size.

LEMON SALSA Peel lemon and finely chop flesh. Transfer any juice and lemon flesh to a medium bowl with remaining ingredients. Stir to combine. Season to taste.

SERVES 4

PREP + COOK TIME 35 MINUTES (+ REFRIGERATION & HEATING)

TANDOORI ZUCCHINI

½ cup (140g) Greek yoghurt

2 cloves garlic, crushed

1 tsp finely grated fresh ginger

1 tbsp tandoori spice mix

6 small zucchini (540g), halved lengthways

20g (¾oz) ghee

4 sprigs fresh curry leaves

SPROUTED CHAAT

400g (12½oz) can chickpeas (garbanzo beans), drained

2 tsp chaat masala spice mix (see tips)

1 tsp cumin seeds

20g (¾oz) ghee

1 tbsp tamarind puree (see tips)

2 tbsp brown sugar

1⅓ cups (200g) crunchy combo sprout mix

2 green onions (scallions), sliced thinly

⅓ cup coarsely chopped coriander (cilantro)

⅓ cup (50g) pomegranate seeds

GARLIC YOGHURT

1 cup (280g) Greek yoghurt

1 small clove garlic, crushed

Combine yoghurt, garlic, ginger and tandoori spice mix in a large bowl. Add zucchini and toss to coat. Season. Refrigerate for 1 hour to marinate.

Prepare a charcoal barbecue to medium heat according to instructions on pages 10-11.

Heat ghee in a medium frying pan over medium-high heat; cook curry leaves for 1 minute or until crisp. Transfer to a plate lined with paper towel.

Make sprouted chaat, then garlic yoghurt.

Cook zucchini on grill over hot coals for 4 minutes each side or until charred lightly and tender.

Top zucchini with sprouted chaat. Drizzle with garlic yoghurt and serve with fried curry leaves.

SPROUTED CHAAT Combine chickpeas, chaat masala mix and cumin seeds in a medium bowl. Season. Return frying pan to medium-high heat with ghee. Cook chickpea mixture for 5 minutes or until golden. Remove from the heat. Heat tamarind, sugar and ¼ cup (60ml) water in a small saucepan over medium heat. Cook for 5 minutes or until thick and sugar has dissolved. Cool dressing. Add sprouts, green onion, coriander, pomegranate seeds and tamarind dressing to the chickpeas. Toss to combine. Season to taste.

GARLIC YOGHURT Combine yoghurt and garlic in a small bowl. Season to taste.

TIPS Use small zucchinis for a better texture and sweet flavour. Chaat masala spice blend is available from the Indian section of supermarkets or Indian grocers. Tamarind puree varies from brand to brand, add more or less, like you would salt for seasoning, depending on taste preference.

SERVES *4*

PREP + COOK TIME 40 MINUTES (+ HEATING)

SUMAC-GRILLED LAMB CUTLETS WITH SMOKY CHARRED EGGPLANT

- **2 large eggplants (1kg)**
- **1 small clove garlic, crushed**
- **1 tbsp finely grated lemon rind**
- **2 tbsp lemon juice**
- **⅓ cup (80ml) extra virgin olive oil**
- **1 tbsp ground sumac**
- **1 tbsp smoked paprika**
- **1 tsp coriander seeds, crushed coarsely**
- **12 lamb cutlets (745g), french-trimmed**
- **250g (8oz) cherry tomatoes, halved and quartered**
- **400g (12½oz) can chickpeas (garbanzo beans), drained, rinsed**
- **1 eschalot (25g), chopped finely**
- **½ cup dill, chopped, plus extra sprigs to serve**

Prepare a charcoal barbecue with hood to high heat according to instructions on pages 10-11.

Prick eggplant all over several times with the tip of a skewer. Cook on grill, turning frequently for 15 minutes, or until completely charred all over. Transfer to a colander placed in a bowl. Cool slightly.

Cut eggplant in half lengthways and scoop out flesh; transfer to a large bowl, discarding skin. Stir in garlic, lemon rind and juice, and half the oil. Season to taste.

Combine sumac, paprika, coriander and the remaining oil in a small bowl. Reserve 2 tablespoons of spice mixture. Rub cutlets all over with remaining mixture. Cook cutlets on grill for 6 minutes, turning halfway, until charred and cooked through. Brush with reserved spice mixture.

Combine tomatoes, chickpeas, eschalot and dill in a small bowl. Season to taste.

To serve, spoon eggplant onto a serving platter. Top with tomato mixture and lamb. Scatter with extra dill.

RUBS

CAJUN RUB

PREP TIME 5 minutes
MAKES ¼ cup

Combine 1½ tbsp mild paprika, 3 tsp dried basil leaves, 1 tsp each ground black pepper and ground fennel seeds, ½ tsp each dried thyme and ground white pepper and a pinch chilli powder (or to taste).

GOES WITH Beef, chicken, lamb and pork.

INDIAN-STYLE RUB

PREP TIME 5 minutes
MAKES ¼ cup

Place 2 tbsp each of coriander seeds and cumin seeds in a small dry frying pan over medium heat; toast, stirring, for 40 seconds or until fragrant. Cool. Using a mortar and pestle, grind seeds finely. Stir in 2 tsp each ground turmeric and medium-hot curry powder and 1 tsp each ground ginger and chilli powder.

GOES WITH Chicken and seafood.

SMOKY PEPPER SALT

PREP TIME 5 minutes
MAKES ¼ cup

Combine 1 tsp mustard powder, 1 tbsp light brown sugar, 1 tsp cracked black pepper, 1 tbsp smoked paprika, ½ tsp cayenne pepper and 2 tsp sea salt in a small bowl.

GOES WITH Beef, chicken, lamb and pork.

41

MAKES *12*

PREP + COOK TIME 40 MINUTES (+ HEATING & REFRIGERATION)

LEMONGRASS PRAWN STICKS WITH CHILLI DIPPING SAUCE

500g (1lb) skinless, boneless flathead fillets, chopped

⅓ cup (100g) Thai red curry paste

2 makrut lime leaves, stem removed, shredded thinly

2 cloves garlic, chopped finely

1 egg

500g (1lb) medium green prawns, peeled, cut into 1cm (½in) pieces

12 small thin lemongrass stalks, trimmed (20cm/8in long)

peanut oil, to brush

CHILLI DIPPING SAUCE

1 tbsp peanut oil

2 tsp sesame oil

3 eschalots (75g), chopped finely

1 tbsp finely grated ginger

120g (4oz) chilli paste in soybean oil

½ tsp finely grated lime rind

1 tbsp lime juice

2 tbsp finely chopped coriander (cilantro), plus extra leaves to serve

Prepare a charcoal barbecue to medium heat according to instructions on pages 10-11.

Place fish, curry paste, lime leaves, garlic and egg in a large food processor; pulse until finely chopped and combined. Transfer mixture to a bowl. Fold in prawns until well combined. Season.

Using slightly damp hands, divide mixture into 12 portions and form into 10cm (4in) logs. Insert a lemongrass stalk through the log lengthways. Place on a tray lined with baking paper. Refrigerate for 30 minutes or until firm.

Meanwhile, make chilli dipping sauce.

Brush skewers with peanut oil. Cook skewers on grill for 12 minutes, turning occasionally or until charred lightly and cooked through.

Serve skewers with dipping sauce, topped with extra coriander.

CHILLI DIPPING SAUCE Heat peanut and sesame oils in a small saucepan over medium-high heat. Add eschalots and ginger; cook, stirring occasionally, for 5 minutes or until eschalots have softened. Stir in chilli paste and ½ cup (125ml) water until combined. Transfer mixture to a high-speed blender; blend until combined. Season to taste. When ready to serve, stir in lime rind, juice and chopped coriander.

TIPS Swap lemongrass 'skewers' with bamboo or metal skewers. You can divide the fish mixture into 24 portions to make smaller party appetisers.

SERVES 4

PREP + COOK TIME 30 MINUTES (+ HEATING)

SNAPPER WITH CHORIZO AND GREEN TOMATO SALSA

—

2 x 400g (12½oz) whole snappers, cleaned

extra virgin olive oil, to drizzle

SHERRY DRESSING

¼ cup (60ml) sherry vinegar

2½ tsp caster (superfine) sugar

2½ tbsp Dijon mustard

½ cup (125ml) extra virgin olive oil

GREEN TOMATO SALSA

2 tbsp extra virgin olive oil

4 eschalots (100g), shaved thinly

3 cloves garlic, grated finely

2 cured chorizo (340g), cut into 1cm (½in) rounds

1½ tbsp coarsely chopped basil

1½ tbsp coarsely chopped dill

1½ tbsp coarsely chopped flat-leaf parsley leaves

6 green tomatoes (500g), chopped coarsely

Prepare a charcoal barbecue with hood to high heat according to instructions on pages 10-11.

Meanwhile, make sherry dressing, then green tomato salsa.

Drizzle snapper all over with oil and place in a fish grilling basket. Place fish on grill; cover with hood. Cook for 7 minutes or until skin is blistered and charred. Lift hood. Turn fish over and cook for another 7 minutes or until fish is almost cooked through. Transfer fish to a tray. Rest for 5 minutes. Repeat with second snapper.

Serve snapper with salsa; drizzle with remaining dressing.

SHERRY DRESSING Whisk ingredients in a small bowl until combined. Season to taste.

GREEN TOMATO SALSA Heat oil in a large frying pan over high heat. Cook eschalot, garlic and chorizo, stirring occasionally, for 5 minutes or until eschalot has softened and chorizo is lightly charred. Add herbs and tomato; cook, tossing, for 1 minute or until warmed through. Process in a small food processor until coarsely chopped. Transfer to a small bowl. Stir in half the sherry dressing and season to taste.

SERVES 6

PREP + COOK TIME 50 MINUTES (+ STANDING, REFRIGERATION & HEATING)

ORUK KEBABS WITH SOUR CHERRY RICE SALAD

½ cup (100g) wild rice

⅓ cup (60g) fine bulgur wheat

1½ cups (300g) basmati rice, rinsed

1kg (2lb) minced (ground) lamb

1 medium onion (150g), chopped

6 cloves garlic, crushed

1 tbsp ground cumin

1 tbsp dried mint

2 tbsp Aleppo pepper (see tips)

1 tbsp finely grated lemon rind

½ cup coarsely chopped dill

1 cup coarsely chopped flat-leaf parsley

¾ cup (115g) dried sour cherries

½ cup (70g) pistachios, toasted

1 tbsp lemon juice

⅓ cup (80ml) extra virgin olive oil, plus extra to brush

store-bought tzatziki, to serve

Cook wild rice in a small saucepan of boiling salted water for 45 minutes or until tender. Drain; rinse under cold running water. Set aside to cool completely.

Meanwhile, place bulgur in a heatproof bowl. Cover with ¼ cup (60ml) boiling water. Stand, covered, for 15 minutes. Fluff with a fork. Set aside to cool completely.

Place basmati rice with 2¼ cups (560ml) water in a medium saucepan over medium heat. Bring to the boil. Reduce heat to low. Cook, covered, for 15 minutes or until liquid is absorbed. Remove from heat. Stand, covered, for 10 minutes. Fluff with a fork. Set aside to cool completely.

Process bulgur, lamb, onion, garlic, cumin, mint, half the Aleppo pepper, half the lemon rind and ¼ cup (60ml) water until mixture is combined and tacky. Season. Divide mixture into 12 portions. Using wet hands, shape portions into 12cm (4¾in) long log shapes. Thread metal skewers lengthways into logs. Place onto a tray; refrigerate for 30 minutes to firm.

Meanwhile, prepare a charcoal barbecue to medium heat according to instructions on pages 10-11.

Combine both rices, dill, parsley, cherries, pistachios, lemon juice, oil, remaining Aleppo pepper and remaining lemon rind in a large bowl. Season to taste.

Brush kebabs with extra oil. Cook kebabs on grill for 12 minutes, turning occasionally or until charred lightly and cooked through.

Serve kebabs with rice salad and tzatziki.

TIPS Aleppo pepper can be replaced with 1 tablespoon chilli flakes. Dried sour cherries can be replaced with dried cranberries soaked in ½ cup red wine vinegar for 1 hour.

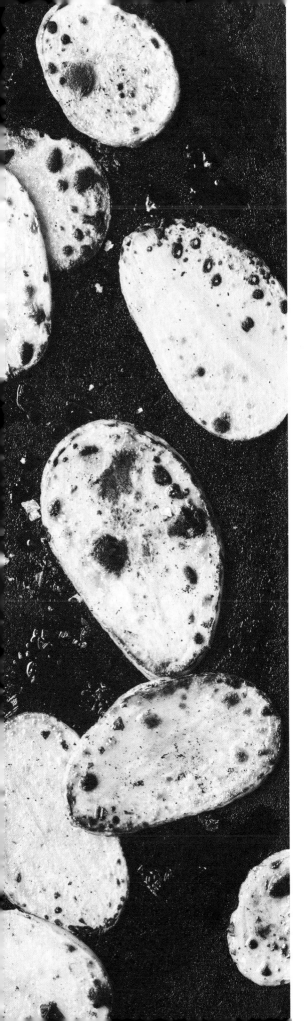

SERVES 8 (AS A SIDE)

PREP + COOK TIME 25 MINUTES (+ HEATING)

LEBANESE POTATOES WITH TOUM (GARLIC SAUCE)

---

6 medium potatoes (1.2kg), scrubbed
2 tbsp extra virgin olive oil
salt flakes, to serve

TOUM
8 cloves garlic
1 tsp sea salt flakes
½ cup (125ml) light olive oil
2 tsp lemon juice

Prepare a charcoal barbecue with a flat plate to medium heat according to instructions on pages 10-11.

Make toum.

Cut potatoes into 5mm (¼in) slices; coat in oil. Season. Cook potatoes on flat plate for 6 minutes each side or until charred and tender.

Serve potatoes with toum. Sprinkle with salt flakes.

TOUM Using a mortar and pestle, pound garlic and salt until an almost smooth paste forms. Slowly add the oil in a steady stream, stirring vigorously with the pestle, until the mixture is light, creamy and thick. Stir in lemon juice.

49

SERVES *4*

PREP + COOK TIME 35 MINUTES (+ HEATING)

BLISTERED TOMATO AND HARISSA PASTA

- **500g (1lb) cherry truss tomatoes**
- **2 medium red onions (340g), cut into wedges**
- **¼ cup (60ml) extra virgin olive oil, plus extra to drizzle**
- **400g (12½oz) rigatoni pasta**
- **1 tbsp harissa paste**
- **⅓ cup (90g) sun-dried tomato pesto**
- **2 tbsp lemon juice**
- **150g (4½oz) firm ricotta, crumbled**
- **½ cup flat-leaf parsley, chopped finely**
- **1 tbsp honey**

Prepare a charcoal barbecue to high heat according to instructions on pages 10-11.

Combine tomatoes, onion and oil in a medium bowl. Season. Cook onion on grill, turning occasionally, for 4 minutes or until lightly charred. Set aside. Cook tomatoes on grill for 5 minutes, turning halfway, until blistered and charred. Remove from grill.

Meanwhile, cook pasta in a large saucepan of boiling salted water until tender. Reserve ½ cup (125ml) cooking water. Drain.

Whisk harissa, pesto and lemon juice in a small bowl until combined. Return pasta and cooking water to saucepan with harissa mixture, onions and half the tomatoes. Set pan over medium heat; gently toss to coat and heat through.

Divide pasta among bowls. Top with remaining tomatoes, the ricotta and parsley. Drizzle with honey.

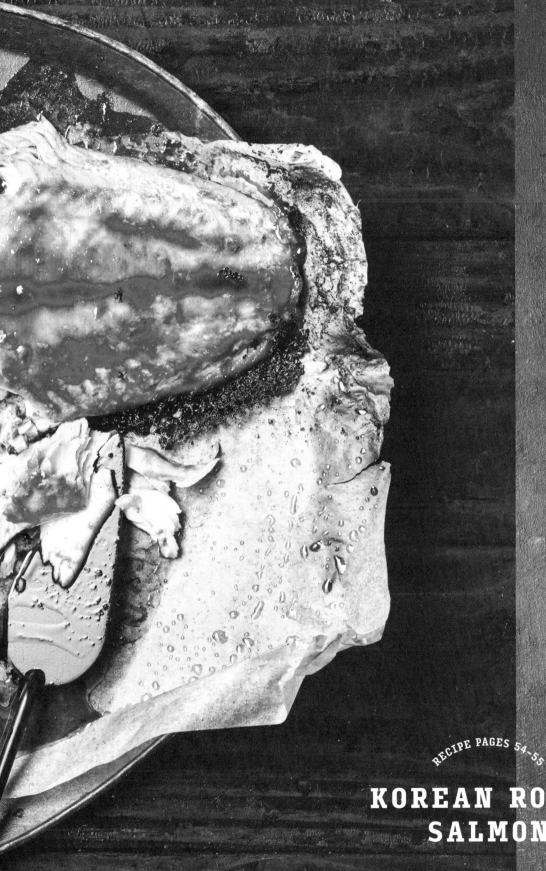

RECIPE PAGES 54-55

KOREAN ROAST SALMON

SERVES *6*

PREP + COOK TIME 50 MINUTES (+ HEATING & STANDING)

KOREAN ROAST SALMON

———

THIS IS A BEAUTIFUL DISH THAT PAIRS THE BRIGHT
AND PUNCHY FLAVOURS OF KOREAN CUISINE WITH
THE RICH FATTINESS OF A FULL SIDE OF SALMON.
SERVE WITH FRESHLY STEAMED SHORT-GRAIN RICE
AND PLENTY OF BANCHAN (KOREAN SIDE DISHES).

1.2kg (2½lb) side of salmon, skin-on, pinboned

60g (2oz) gochujang (Korean chilli paste)

125g (4oz) Korean barbecue bulgogi sauce (see tip)

2 tbsp brown sugar

2 tsp finely grated ginger

baby red shiso and lime halves, to serve

QUICK PICKLED CUCUMBER

¼ cup (60ml) lime juice

2 tbsp fish sauce

2 tbsp caster (superfine) sugar

3 cloves garlic, grated finely

600g (1¼lb) qukes (baby cucumbers), sliced thinly into rounds

Prepare a charcoal barbecue with hood to high heat according to instructions on pages 10-11. Temperature should read 250°C/480°F on a thermometer.

Grease an oven tray that is both large enough to fit salmon and fit in your barbecue; line with baking paper. Place salmon, skin-side down, on tray. Season.

Place gochujang, bulgogi sauce, sugar and ginger in a small bowl and whisk until combined. Spread mixture evenly over salmon. Roast salmon in barbecue, with hood closed, for 20 minutes until salmon is cooked to medium or to your liking. Remove; stand for 10 minutes.

Meanwhile, make quick pickled cucumber.

Top serve, top salmon with pickled cucumber and shiso. Serve with lime halves.

QUICK PICKLED CUCUMBER Whisk lime juice, fish sauce, sugar and garlic in a large bowl until combined. Add qukes; toss to combine. Stand for 20 minutes. Adjust seasonings to taste by adding more lime juice, fish sauce or sugar as required.

TIP Gochujang and bulgogi sauce are available in selected supermarkets, specialty food stores and Asian grocers.

SERVES *6*

PREP + COOK TIME 45 MINUTES (+ HEATING)

SKIRT STEAK WITH CHARRED TOMATO AND ESCHALOT SALSA

---

2 large oxheart tomatoes (520g), sliced thickly

6 eschalots (150g), peeled, halved lengthways

1kg (2lb) skirt steak

1 bunch green onions (scallions)

½ cup (125ml) extra virgin olive oil

⅓ cup (80ml) sherry vinegar

1½ tbsp brown sugar

½ cup coarsely chopped coriander (cilantro)

2 cloves garlic, crushed

smoked salt, to serve (optional)

Prepare a charcoal barbecue to high heat according to instructions on pages 10-11.

Cook tomato and eschalots on grill, turning once, for 5 minutes or until charred. Remove from heat; cool.

Season steak. Place steak and green onion on grill. Cook steak for 8 minutes, turning halfway through cooking time, or until charred on the outside and medium-rare in the centre. Cook green onion for 3 minutes, turning occasionally, or until tender and charred. Remove from heat.

Meanwhile, whisk olive oil, vinegar and sugar in a medium bowl until combined and sugar is dissolved. Whisk coriander and garlic into oil mixture. Finely chop cooled tomato and eshalots, and stir into mixture until just combined. Season to taste.

Slice steak; spoon over tomato salsa and serve with charred green onion. Sprinkle with smoked salt.

MAKES *12*

PREP + COOK TIME 50 MINUTES (+ REFRIGERATION & HEATING)

TURMERIC CHICKEN SATAY SKEWERS

---

1 chicken breast fillet (200g)

3 chicken thigh fillets (510g), skin-on

2 stalks lemongrass, white part only

2 eschalots (50g)

30g (1oz) fresh ginger

2 tsp ground turmeric

1 tsp ground cumin

1½ tbsp finely grated palm sugar

1 tsp salt

¼ cup (60ml) vegetable oil

coriander (cilantro) leaves and finely chopped fresh long red chilli, to serve

SATAY SAUCE

2 tbsp vegetable oil

¾ cup (105g) raw peanuts

4 dried chillies, soaked in boiling water for 10 minutes

2 eschalots (50g), peeled, chopped

1 stalk lemongrass, white part only, chopped

3 cloves garlic, chopped

15g (½oz) fresh ginger, chopped

1 tsp tamarind puree

2 tsp kecap manis

1½ tbsp grated palm sugar

Using a meat mallet or rolling pin, pound chicken until 2cm (¾in) thick. Cut into 2cm (¾in) pieces; transfer to a medium bowl.

Coarsely chop lemongrass, eschalots and ginger, then blend with turmeric, cumin, palm sugar, salt and 2 tablespoons of the oil until a thick paste forms. Add paste to chicken and toss to coat. Refrigerate, covered, for 3 hours.

Prepare a charcoal barbecue or hibachi to medium heat according to instructions on pages 10-11.

Meanwhile, make satay sauce.

Combine ¼ cup satay sauce, 1 tablespoon water and remaining oil in a small bowl. Thread chicken evenly onto 12 metal skewers. Cook skewers on grill, turning and brushing occasionally with satay sauce mixture, for 15 minutes or until charred and cooked through.

Top skewers with some of the remaining satay sauce, the coriander leaves and chilli. Serve with pan-fried mushrooms and lettuce leaves, if you like.

SATAY SAUCE Heat oil and peanuts in a medium frying pan over medium-high heat for 5 minutes or until peanuts are deep golden brown. Using a slotted spoon, transfer peanuts to a plate lined with paper towel. Reserve oil in pan. Process peanuts in a small food processor until finely chopped. Drain chillies. Process eschalots, lemongrass, garlic, ginger and chillies with 1 tablespoon water until smooth. Return frying pan with reserved oil to medium-high heat. Cook eschalot mixture, stirring, for 3 minutes or until fragrant. Add tamarind, kecap manis and palm sugar. Cook, stirring for 1 minute or until sugar dissolves. Add chopped peanuts and 1½ cups (375ml) water. Bring to a simmer; cook for 15 minutes or until thickened.

TIP Satay sauce can be made up to 3 days before. Store in an airtight container in the fridge.

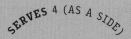

SERVES 4 (AS A SIDE)

PREP + COOK TIME 30 MINUTES (+ HEATING)

GARLIC BUTTER MUSHROOMS WITH LEMON RICOTTA

250g (8oz) unsalted butter, chopped

3 cloves smoked garlic, sliced thinly

½ bunch each rosemary, oregano and thyme, plus extra leaves to serve

300g (9½oz) oyster mushrooms

8 portobello mushrooms (400g)

LEMON RICOTTA

2 cups (480g) firm ricotta

1 tbsp finely grated lemon rind

2 tbsp lemon juice

Prepare a charcoal barbecue with hood to medium heat according to instructions on pages 10-11.

Make lemon ricotta.

Place butter in a medium saucepan; place pan on grill over hot coals until butter is melted. Stir in smoked garlic; leave over the heat for 3 minutes to infuse. Remove from grill.

Tie the herbs together with kitchen string to form a bouquet.

Season mushrooms. Cook mushrooms on grill, turning occasionally, with hood closed, for 15 minutes, basting mushrooms frequently with the garlic butter using the herb bouquet as a brush.

Spoon lemon ricotta onto serving plates; top with mushrooms. Drizzle over any remaining garlic butter. Scatter with extra herbs. Season.

LEMON RICOTTA Whisk ingredients in a large bowl until smooth and combined. Season to taste.

With a firm and steady helping hand, a pile of wood can be transformed into a roaring, glowing fire. There are very few foods that are not improved by the touch of the fire – a little smoky aroma and colour from the grill.

MAKES *14*

PREP + COOK TIME 40 MINUTES (+ HEATING)

CORN FRITTERS COOKED IN CORN HUSKS

---

4 corn cobs (1kg)

1 cup (150g) plain (all-purpose) flour

½ cup (90g) yellow corn (maize) flour (see tips)

1 tsp baking powder

1 egg, beaten lightly

1 cup (250ml) buttermilk

¼ cup chopped chives

½ cup (40g) finely grated parmesan

cooking oil spray

tomato salsa, to serve

Prepare a charcoal barbecue to high heat according to instructions on pages 10-11. (See tips.)

Carefully remove husks from corn cobs, in large intact pieces. You will need 28 pieces. Remove silks; discard.

Cook corn cobs on grill for 8 minutes, turning occasionally, or until slightly charred. When cool enough to handle, cut kernels from cobs.

Blanch husks in a medium saucepan of boiling water for 1 minute. Transfer husks to a large bowl of iced water. Drain well. Pat dry with paper towel.

Combine flours and baking powder in a large bowl. Stir in corn kernels, egg, buttermilk, chives and parmesan until combined. Season with salt and freshly ground black pepper.

One at a time, spoon ¼ cup of the mixture into the centre of a piece of corn husk. Fold in the sides to enclose. Using a second husk, wrap around the parcel in the opposite direction to enclose. Secure with a toothpick.

Lightly spray parcels with cooking oil spray. Cook parcels on grill for 5 minutes each side or until tender and cooked through. To serve, unwrap fritters and top with tomato salsa.

TIPS For effective and even cooking ensure that the grill is set 10cm (4in) above the hot coals. Yellow corn (maize) flour is available from delis and speciality food stores.

SERVES 2

PREP + COOK TIME 25 MINUTES (+ REFRIGERATION, HEATING & STANDING)

MOO NAM TOK
(THAI GRILLED BEEF SALAD)

---

2 tsp light soy sauce

1 tsp freshly ground black pepper

1½ tbsp fish sauce

2 x 250g (8oz) beef scotch fillet steaks

2 tbsp lime juice

2 tsp finely grated palm sugar

2 tsp dried chilli flakes

1 tbsp jasmine rice

1 eschalot (25g), sliced thinly

1 cup mint leaves

1 cup coriander (cilantro) leaves

1 cos (romaine) lettuce, trimmed, leaves separated

100g (3oz) snake beans, chopped

lime wedges, to serve

Combine soy sauce, pepper and 1 tablespoon of the fish sauce in a medium bowl. Add beef; toss to coat. Refrigerate for 1 hour, turning beef over in marinade halfway through.

Meanwhile, prepare a charcoal barbecue to medium heat according to instructions on pages 10-11.

Stir lime juice, palm sugar, chilli and remaining fish sauce in a small bowl until sugar dissolves. Set aside.

Toast rice in a small frying pan over medium-high heat, stirring, for 2 minutes or until golden and fragrant. Using a mortar and pestle, grind toasted rice into a fine powder.

Cook beef on grill for 4 minutes each side or until browned and just cooked through. Transfer to a plate; cover. Rest for 10 minutes. Thinly slice.

Combine beef, eschalot, mint, coriander and toasted rice powder. Drizzle with lime dressing.

Serve beef mixture with cos lettuce, snake beans and lime wedges.

TIP Roasted rice powder (known as khao khua) is a traditional ingredient in this salad but can be left out if you prefer.

RECIPE PAGES 70–71

SUCKLING PIG

SERVES 12

PREP + COOK TIME 5 HOURS 30 MINUTES (+ HEATING)

SUCKLING PIG

A SUCKLING PIG IS THE KING OF BARBECUING PROJECTS – LARGE AND SPECTACULAR-LOOKING, THIS DELICIOUS COOKED MEAT CALLS FOR A SPECIAL OCCASION. TO COOK IT YOU WILL NEED A CHARCOAL SPIT ROTISSERIE SET UP, WHICH CAN BE HIRED, AND TO ORDER A SUCKLING PIG FROM YOUR BUTCHER.

STORING If you have space in your fridge, leave the pig uncovered overnight; this will assist with making the skin crisp. If you don't have space in the fridge, place pig overnight in a cooler with ice bricks or over ice, covered with a tight-fitting lid. Place pig in a clean unscented garbage bag first to ensure that it is not in direct contact with ice.

ROTISSERIE BARBECUE HIRE Search online for a local hire place; these businesses will deliver the barbecue with everything required to your location, including charcoal and spit. Many places will assist, or at least talk you through how to get the pig on the spit.

4 bulbs garlic

5 large onions (850g)

5 large apples (1kg)

1 whole suckling pig (approx. 10kg)

¾ cup (180ml) olive oil

3 small pineapples

1 cup coarsely chopped coriander (cilantro)

GLAZE

1 cup (280g) tomato sauce

1 cup (125ml) soy sauce

⅔ cup (160ml) malt vinegar

2 tbsp finely grated ginger

⅔ cup (150g) firmly packed brown sugar

⅔ cup (160ml) fresh pineapple juice

Prepare the barbecue coals, following the instructions on pages 10-11.

Meanwhile, prepare the pig. Remove 12 cloves of garlic from the bulbs and crush. To make glaze, place half the crushed garlic and the glaze ingredients in a medium saucepan over medium heat; bring to a simmer. Cook for 5 minutes or until thickened slightly. Set aside to cool. Divide glaze in half.

Cut remaining whole bulbs garlic in half horizontally, and the onions and apples into quarters (with skin and seeds). Place pig on a clean work surface and fill pig cavity with the chopped ingredients.

To enclose cavity, thread several metal skewers along both sides of cavity, through the skin. You could also sew it up using butcher's twine and a larding needle, or stainless-steel wire, starting at one end and feeding the wire through both sides.

Pat pig dry with paper towel. Using a very sharp knife, lightly score the skin at 3cm (1¼in) intervals. Combine remaining crushed garlic and the oil. Using your hands, rub oil mixture over the entire pig, then rub the pig with glaze. Make sure to rub both sides of pig with oil and glaze.

Push the sharp end of the rotisserie skewer through the back of the animal and feed it through the inside of the pig, through and out of the mouth, ensuring the animal is centred on the skewer. Feed the back brace underneath the rotisserie skewer, through the top of the pig. To assist with this, make small incisions in the skin with a knife first. The back brace should lock in place with a flat plate which sits outside of the pig with two wingnuts. To secure the legs, some rotisserie set ups will include a leg bracket, but if yours hasn't you will need to secure the hind and front legs closer to the animal's body with wire or butcher string.

Once you have glowing coals, position the pig on the rotisserie. The pig should be set at a sufficient height that

you can hold your hand under the pig for 7 seconds. If you cannot do this, adjust to a little higher. You will need someone to assist attaching the pig on the spit to the rotisserie.

Cook pig, for 5 hours, brushing every hour with any leftover glaze or until it reaches an internal temperature of 75°C/167°F at the thickest part, or when a skewer inserted for 30 seconds feels hot when held to the inside of your wrist. During the cooking process, you will need to add cold charcoal alongside the hot coals to ensure even and continued heat. Start to keep a closer eye on the pig as it colours, you may need to cover the ears or any parts that are browning faster with foil. Or if the whole pig is browning too fast, raise the rotisserie slightly. There are a few variables with the cooking time so be prepared for a faster and longer cooking animal.

During the last hour of cooking, place whole pineapples in the coals for 30-40 minutes; cook pig, rotating until charred.

Remove pineapples from coals. Cut skin from pineapples and chop coarsely; toss with coriander in a medium bowl.

Transfer the pig to a large board, and, using barbecue gloves, remove the rotisserie apparatus from the animal. Carve to serve. Accompany with roast pineapple salsa.

SERVES 4

PREP + COOK TIME 35 MINUTES
(+ REFRIGERATION)

LIMONCELLO GLAZED PINEAPPLE

2 small pineapples (1.8kg) with tops
¾ cup (180ml) limoncello
⅓ cup (75g) firmly packed brown sugar
30g (1oz) butter
vanilla ice-cream, to serve

Remove skin from pineapples using a sharp knife, leaving tops attached; cut lengthways into quarters. Combine limoncello and sugar in a large ceramic dish. Place pineapple quarters in dish; toss to coat in limoncello mixture. Refrigerate, covered, for 1 hour.

Prepare a charcoal barbecue to high heat according to instructions on pages 10-11. Set grill 20cm (8in) above coals.

Drain pineapple, reserving marinade. Place the marinade in a medium saucepan over hot coals; bring to the boil. Reduce heat; simmer for 5 minutes or until reduced and syrupy. (Keep your face away from the pan as the syrup may ignite; if this happens, leave until the alcohol burns off, about 1 minute). Remove from heat; whisk in butter until melted and combined.

Cook pineapple on grill for 20 minutes, brushing occasionally with half the marinade and turning, until golden and lightly charred. Serve with ice-cream, drizzled with remaining marinade.

SERVES *8*

PREP + COOK TIME 45 MINUTES (+ HEATING & REFRIGERATION)

CAST IRON GOLDEN
SYRUP PUDDING

1½ cups (225g) plain (all-purpose) flour

1 tbsp baking powder

¼ cup (55g) caster (superfine) sugar

½ tsp sea salt flakes

60g (2oz) cold butter, chopped

225ml milk

1 tsp vanilla bean paste

300ml pouring cream

¾ cup (205g) golden syrup

ORANGE BLOSSOM CREAM

½ cup (120g) sour cream

½ cup (120g) thick (double) cream

1½ tsp orange blossom water

Prepare a charcoal barbecue with hood to low-medium heat according to instructions on pages 10-11. Temperature should read about 170°C/340°F on a thermometer.

Lightly grease a 5cm (2in) deep, 25cm (10in) round cast iron pan.

Combine flour, baking powder, sugar and salt in a large bowl. Using your fingertips, rub butter into flour until mixture resembles fine breadcrumbs. Add milk and vanilla, stir until combined. Spoon mixture into prepared pan. Refrigerate for 30 minutes.

Place cream and golden syrup in a medium saucepan over medium heat. Bring to a gentle simmer. Cook for 2 minutes. Carefully pour mixture over batter in cast iron pan.

Place cast iron pan on grill. Cover with hood. Cook for 30 minutes or until pudding is set and a skewer inserted into the centre comes out clean.

Meanwhile, make orange blossom cream.

Serve pudding warm, topped with dollops of orange blossom cream.

ORANGE BLOSSOM CREAM Whisk ingredients in a medium bowl until soft peaks form. Refrigerate until ready to serve.

TIP Instead of making the orange blossom cream, you can serve pudding with plain thick (double) cream or vanilla ice-cream.

SERVES *4*

PREP + COOK TIME 15 MINUTES (+ FREEZING)

GRILLED APRICOTS WITH HALVA ICE-CREAM

500ml (2 cups) vanilla ice-cream, softened

100g (3oz) pistachio halva, chopped (see tip)

8 ripe apricots (400g), halved, pitted

1 tbsp extra virgin olive oil

½ tsp salt flakes

¼ cup (40g) pistachios, toasted, chopped

honey, to serve

Place ice-cream and halva in a medium metal bowl and fold until just combined. Cover directly with plastic wrap. Freeze for at least 2 hours or overnight.

Prepare a charcoal barbecue to medium heat according to instructions on pages 10-11.

Toss apricots, oil and salt in a medium bowl until well coated; thread onto skewers.

Cook apricots on grill for 2 minutes each side or until charred and softened.

Divide ice-cream among bowls. Top with warm apricots. Sprinkle with pistachios and drizzle with honey to serve.

TIP Halva is Middle Eastern confectionery made from ground sesame seeds. It is available in tubs from delis and Middle Eastern food stores.

GRILL

THERE'S A REASON THAT BARBECUING IS EVERYONE'S
FAVOURITE WAY TO CELEBRATE. THERE'S NOT MUCH
THAT CAN'T BE IMPROVED BY A STINT ON THE GRILL,
THOSE DISTINCTIVE CHAR MARKS AND BARBECUE
FLAVOURS ARE A GUARANTEED CROWD PLEASER.

HOW TO COOK THE PERFECT STEAK

PERFECT STEAK

Preheat a heavy-based frying pan, char-grill pan or barbecue over a high heat until hot. Brush or rub steaks with olive oil. Season with a little salt and freshly ground black pepper. Cook steaks over high heat to your liking, following instructions opposite. Turn steaks once using tongs, not a fork.
To test if steak is ready, use the blunt end of the tongs to press the meat in the thickest part. Remove steak from the heat, cover with foil and rest for 5 minutes; this will make the steak more tender. Serve steak with pan juices and wholegrain mustard.

RARE Cook for a few minutes per side, depending on thickness. Cook until steak feels very soft when pressed with tongs.

MEDIUM RARE Cook for a few minutes per side, depending on thickness. Cook until steak gives slight resistance towards the middle, but springs back when pressed with tongs.

MEDIUM Cook on one side until moisture is pooling on top. Cook on second side until surface moisture is visible. Cook until steak feels springy when pressed with tongs.

WELL DONE Cook on one side until moisture is pooling on top. Cook on second side until moisture is pooling on top. Reduce heat slightly; cook until steak feels very firm when pressed.

SERVES 6

PREP + COOK TIME 1 HOUR 10 MINUTES (+ REFRIGERATION)

PERUVIAN-STYLE BUTTERFLIED CHICKEN WITH GREEN SAUCE

1 tbsp coriander seeds

1 tbsp cumin seeds

2 tsp whole cloves

1 tbsp ground cinnamon

1 tbsp freshly ground
   black pepper

½ cup (125ml) extra virgin
   olive oil

6 cloves garlic, crushed

1.6kg (3½lb) whole chicken,
   butterflied

2 limes (130g), halved

GREEN SAUCE

1 cup (300g) whole-egg
   mayonnaise

1 bunch coriander (cilantro),
   tough stems removed

2 yellow bullhorn peppers,
   chopped, seeds removed

2 fresh jalapeño chillies, halved,
   seeds removed

⅓ cup (80g) finely grated
   parmesan

¼ cup (60ml) lime juice

1 small clove garlic, crushed

Place a small frying pan over medium heat. Add seeds and cloves; toast for 2 minutes, stirring frequently, until fragrant. Using a mortar and pestle, grind spices until finely crushed. Stir in cinnamon and pepper. Transfer to a small bowl.

Stir oil and garlic into spices until combined. Rub half the mixture all over chicken. Place chicken, uncovered, in fridge, for 1 hour to slightly dry out skin.

Remove chicken from fridge and bring to room temperature. Meanwhile, heat a covered gas barbecue with all burners set to high and hood closed, until temperature reaches 250°C/485°F on a thermometer.

Place chicken, skin-side down, on grill; cook for 2 minutes. Set burners to low. Close hood. Cook chicken for a further 25 minutes.

Meanwhile, make green sauce.

Turn chicken over. Close hood; cook for a further 15 minutes, basting occasionally with remaining marinade. Open hood and cook for a further 5 minutes or until chicken is tender and cooked through. Transfer to a plate. Rest for 10 minutes before serving.

Meanwhile, cook lime halves on grill, cut-side down, for 1 minute or until charred and grill marks appear.

Serve chicken, cut into pieces, with green sauce and limes.

GREEN SAUCE Process ingredients in a food processor or high-speed blender until very smooth. Refrigerate, covered, until ready to serve.

SERVES *4*

PREP + COOK TIME 45 MINUTES (+ STANDING)

VEGIE OLIVE OIL FLATBREADS

---

2 cups (300g) bread flour

1¼ tsp dried yeast

1 tsp sea salt flakes

¾ cup (180ml) extra virgin olive oil

¾ cup (180ml) lukewarm water

4 cloves black garlic (see tip)

1 clove garlic, peeled

⅓ cup firmly packed flat-leaf parsley leaves, plus extra sprigs to serve

400g (12½oz) king brown mushrooms, cut lengthways into thick slices

1 medium red onion (170g), cut into thick rounds

200g (6½oz) haloumi, grated coarsely

250g (8oz) cherry truss tomatoes

Heat a covered gas barbecue with outside burners set to low and hood closed.

Combine flour, yeast and salt in a large bowl; make a well in the centre. Stir in ¼ cup (60ml) of the oil and enough of the water for a soft dough to form. Knead dough on a floured surface for 10 minutes or until smooth and elastic.

Place dough in a large, oiled bowl; carefully cover with a clean tea towel. Stand on a raised rack on the barbecue, hood closed for 2 hours or until nearly doubled in size. Turn dough out onto a lightly floured surface. Knead dough until smooth. Increase barbecue burners to high.

Using a mortar and pestle, pound both garlics, parsley and ¼ cup (60ml) of the oil until well combined. Season to taste.

Toss mushrooms and onion with remaining oil in a large bowl. Cook over direct heat on the barbecue flat plate for 5 minutes, turning, until golden and softened. Reduce all burners of barbecue to medium.

Divide dough into two portions. Roll each portion into a 20cm x 30cm (8in x 12in) oval. Spread with the garlic paste; top with mushrooms, onion and haloumi. Cook over direct heat on the flat plate, hood closed, for 15 minutes. Top with tomatoes. Close lid and cook a further 10 minutes or until base is crisp and top is golden. Serve immediately, topped with extra parsley.

TIP Black garlic is temperature-controlled aged garlic. Aged in specific conditions for a period of weeks or months, it transforms into a striking black colour, which is sticky, sweet and mild in flavour. Black garlic is available from delis and green grocers.

SERVES 4 (AS A SIDE)

PREP + COOK TIME 20 MINUTES

GRILLED BROCCOLI WITH SPINACH HUMMUS

1 large head broccoli (500g), quartered

300g (9½oz) English spinach, washed, chopped

400g (12½oz) can chickpeas (garbanzo beans), drained, rinsed

1 clove garlic

½ cup (140g) tahini

¼ cup (60ml) lemon juice

¼ cup (60ml) extra virgin olive oil, plus extra to serve

1 tsp ground cumin

⅓ cup (45g) roasted skinned hazelnuts, chopped coarsely

Heat a covered gas barbecue with all burners set to high and hood closed.

Meanwhile, blanch broccoli in a large saucepan of boiling salted water for 2 minutes. Transfer immediately to a large bowl of iced water. Reserve blanching water off the heat.

Place spinach in reserved hot water; stand for 30 seconds and drain. Rinse spinach under cold water, then squeeze out most of the excess liquid.

To make spinach hummus, place spinach, chickpeas, garlic, tahini, lemon juice, 1 tablespoon of the oil and the cumin in a high-speed blender; blend until very smooth. Season to taste.

Brush remaining oil over cut-side of broccoli; season. Reduce burners to medium heat. Cook broccoli on grill, for 1 minute each side or until charred.

Spread spinach hummus over the base of a serving plate. Top with broccoli. Drizzle with extra oil and scatter with hazelnuts.

SERVES 6
(AS A STARTER)

PREP + COOK TIME 30 MINUTES

BRIE WHEEL FONDUE WITH GRILLED CRUDITÉS

500g (1lb) wheel of brie

2 cloves garlic, sliced

400g (12½oz) rainbow Dutch carrots, trimmed, halved lengthways

2 bunches asparagus (340g), trimmed, halved lengthways

2 tbsp extra virgin olive oil, plus extra to brush

½ ciabatta (220g), sliced thinly

SALSA VERDE

½ cup basil leaves

½ cup mint leaves

1 tbsp baby capers

1 tsp finely grated lemon rind

¼ cup (60ml) lemon juice

¼ cup (60ml) extra virgin olive oil

Make salsa verde.

Heat a covered gas barbecue with all burners set to high and hood closed. Unwrap cheese and place in a 20cm (8in) cast-iron pan. Score top in a cross-hatch pattern and press garlic slices into cuts.

Place carrots and asparagus in a large bowl. Season. Add oil, toss to combine.

Place the cheese on the edge of the grill away from direct heat. Cook for 10 minutes, with hood closed, or until soft, melted and lightly browned.

Add carrots to grill. Cook for 4 minutes, turning occasionally, until charred and tender-crisp. Add asparagus to grill. Cook, turning occasionally, for 3 minutes or until charred and tender-crisp. Add ciabatta to grill. Cook both sides until toasted.

Drizzle cheese with salsa verde. Serve with grilled crudités and toasted bread.

SALSA VERDE Place ingredients in a blender; blend until smooth. Season to taste.

SERVES *2*

PREP + COOK TIME 30 MINUTES (+ REFRIGERATION)

BÚN THIT (RICE VERMICELLI AND GRILLED PORK)

---

1 stalk lemongrass, white part only, chopped coarsely

1 eschalot (25g), peeled, chopped

2 cloves garlic

2 fresh small red chillies, plus extra sliced, to serve

2 tbsp fish sauce, plus extra to serve

1 tbsp oyster sauce

¼ cup (90g) honey

¼ cup (60ml) vegetable oil, plus extra for greasing

300g (9½oz) boneless pork shoulder, sliced very thinly

2 tbsp rice wine vinegar

1 large carrot (180g), peeled, julienned

2 green onions (scallions), sliced thinly

125g (4oz) dried rice vermicelli noodles

½ cup each mint and Vietnamese mint leaves

1 Lebanese cucumber (130g), sliced into batons

½ cup (125ml) Vietnamese dipping sauce

Blend or process lemongrass, eschalot, garlic, chillies, fish and oyster sauces, 2 tablespoons of the honey and 1 tablespoon of the oil in a small food processor until finely chopped. Transfer to a medium bowl. Add pork; toss to coat. Refrigerate for 30 minutes.

Meanwhile, heat vinegar and remaining honey with 2 tablespoons water in a small saucepan over medium heat until honey dissolves. Pour into a small bowl; cool. Add carrot and stir to combine.

Return cleaned saucepan to medium-high heat. Add remaining oil; heat until oil is shimmering. Add half of the green onion and cook for 30 seconds or until softened. Remove saucepan from heat. Set aside for infused oil to cool.

Heat a covered gas barbecue with all burners set to medium-high and hood closed. Soak vermicelli in boiling water for 5 minutes. Drain. Rinse under cold running water.

Oil a barbecue grilling basket; place pork in a single layer in basket. Cook on grill, for 6 minutes each side or until caramelised and cooked through.

To serve, drain carrot. Divide noodles between serving bowls. Top with pork, carrot, remaining green onion, green onion oil, mint and cucumbers. Serve with dipping sauce, combined with extra sliced chilli and extra fish sauce.

TIPS Thinly sliced pork is available from Asian grocers or ask your butcher to slice it thinly for you. You can use all mint instead of the Vietnamese mint, if preferred.

RECIPE PAGES 94–95

CELERIAC
SHAWARMA

SERVES *4*

PREP + COOK TIME 1 HOUR 35 MINUTES

CELERIAC SHAWARMA

———————

SHAWARMA, TRADITIONALLY A MIDDLE EASTERN DISH MADE WITH THIN SLICES OF LAMB, CHICKEN OR BEEF STACKED HORIZONTALLY, IS GIVEN A CLEVER VEGAN TWIST HERE USING THE VERSATILE ROOT VEGETABLE CELERIAC. SHAVE WITH A SHARP KNIFE TO SERVE.

10g (½oz) dried porcini
    mushrooms

2 tbsp baharat

2 tsp sweet paprika

2 tsp freshly ground
    black pepper

1 tsp ground turmeric

5 cloves garlic, crushed

1 tbsp tomato paste

1 tbsp lemon juice

½ cup (125ml) extra virgin
    olive oil

3 celeriac (celery root)
    (1.8kg), peeled, cut into
    4mm (¼in) slices (see tips)

cooking oil spray

Lebanese bread, store-bought
    hummus and flat-leaf
    parsley leaves, to serve

BASTING SAUCE

1 tbsp apple cider vinegar

2 tbsp extra virgin olive oil

1 tbsp baharat

1 tbsp date molasses

Heat a covered gas barbecue with all burners set to low and hood closed.

Using a spice grinder or high-speed blender, grind porcini into a fine powder. Transfer to a large bowl with baharat, paprika, pepper, turmeric, garlic, tomato paste, lemon juice and olive oil. Stir to combine. Season generously with salt. Add celeriac and toss to coat.

Thread celeriac onto a long thick skewer (see tips), pressing slices tightly together to compact. Lay two pieces of foil together and lightly spray with oil. Sit celeriac skewer in centre and wrap tightly to enclose.

Cook celeriac on grill, with hood closed, for 1 hour, turning skewer 90 degrees every 15 minutes, until celeriac has softened.

Meanwhile, make basting sauce.

Carefully unwrap celeriac; brush all over with basting sauce. Continue to cook celeriac directly on grill for a further 15 minutes, turning and basting regularly until charred all over.

To serve, shave slices from celeriac skewer. Serve with bread, hummus and parsley.

BASTING SAUCE Whisk ingredients in a medium jug until combined.

TIPS Use a mandoline to cut the celeriac. If you don't have a thick skewer, thread celeriac onto 4 metal skewers bundled together.

SERVES 4

PREP + COOK TIME 25 MINUTES

POTATO AND CHORIZO SALAD WITH CORIANDER PESTO

_____

1 kg (2lb) kipfler (fingerling) potatoes, scrubbed

1 tbsp extra virgin olive oil

2 cured chorizo (200g), sliced thinly on the diagonal

180g (5½oz) mixed salad leaves

2 tbsp dill sprigs

PESTO

1 cup coriander (cilantro) leaves

½ cup flat-leaf parsley leaves

1 tsp ground coriander

1 clove garlic, crushed

¼ cup (60ml) lemon juice

⅓ cup (80ml) extra virgin olive oil

Boil potatoes in large saucepan of boiling salted water for 10 minutes or until tender. Drain.

Make pesto. Heat a covered gas barbecue with all burners set to high and hood closed.

Cut potatoes in half lengthways and drizzle with oil. Cook on grill, turning occasionally, for 8 minutes or until lightly charred. Add chorizo to grill; cook for 4 minutes, turning occasionally or until golden. Remove from heat. Cool slightly.

Serve grilled potatoes and chorizo with salad leaves and dill, drizzled with pesto.

PESTO Place ingredients in a small blender; blend until smooth. Season to taste.

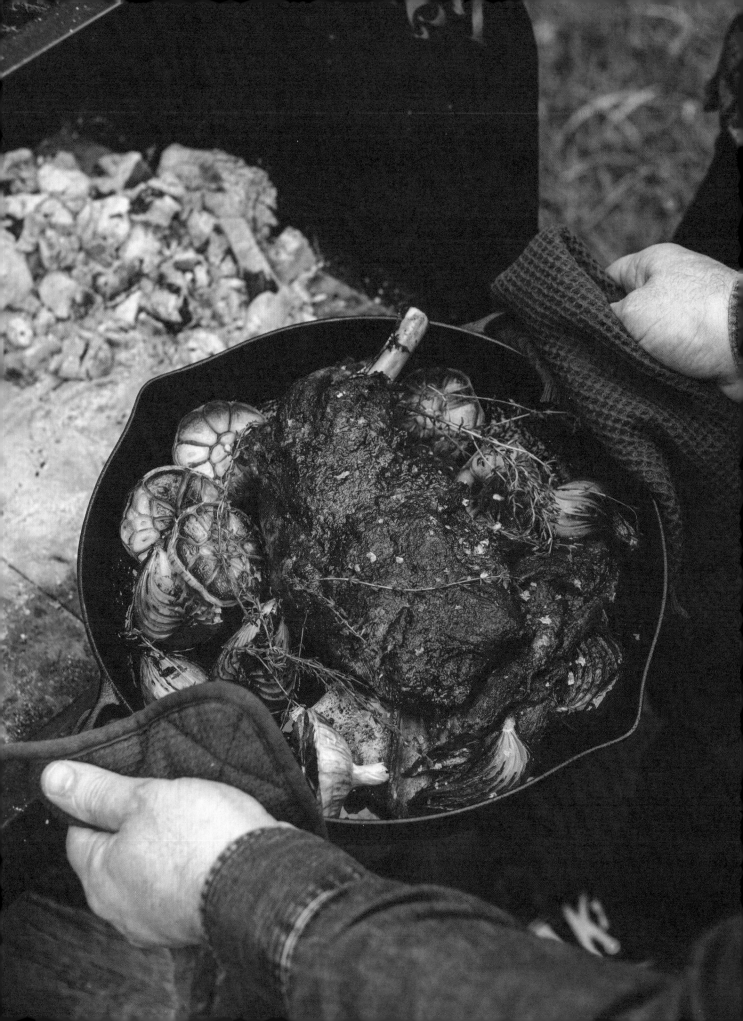

SERVES 4

PREP + COOK TIME 7 HOURS

SLOW-COOKED LAMB SHOULDER

2.4kg (4¾lb) lamb shoulder,
   shank on

6 cloves garlic, peeled, quartered

2 tsp olive oil

2 garlic bulbs (140g), extra,
   halved horizontally

2 medium red onions (340g),
   unpeeled, cut into wedges

2 tbsp pomegranate molasses

1½ tbsp berbere spice mix
   (see Glossary, page 180)

2 tsp ground cumin

1 tsp salt flakes

1½ cups (375ml) chicken stock

6 sprigs thyme

Place a large cast iron frying pan in a covered gas barbecue
with outside burners set to medium and hood closed.

Cut 2cm (¾in) slits into lamb and press garlic quarters into
incisions. Rub lamb with oil.

Once frying pan is hot, add lamb, fat-side down; cook with hood
open, for 5 minutes or until well browned. Turn lamb over and
repeat for other side. Transfer lamb to a tray. Add extra garlic bulbs
and the onion, cut-side down, to the rendered lamb fat in the pan;
cook for 2 minutes or until blackened slightly, then turn over.

Remove the pan from barbecue. Rub lamb with pomegranate
molasses, then sprinkle with combined berbere spice mix,
ground cumin and salt.

Move onion and garlic to the side of the pan and place lamb,
seasoned-side up, in the centre. Pour stock around the lamb,
then cover very tightly with foil.

Return lamb to the barbecue; cook with the hood closed for
6 hours or until meat is falling from the bones.

Serve lamb scattered with thyme sprigs and extra salt.

TIPS You can stud the lamb with garlic a day ahead. Leaving
the skin on the onions and garlic keeps them intact during
cooking. If you like, strain the cooking juices and squeeze the
garlic from the cloves for a garlic jus.

SERVES 4

PREP + COOK TIME 15 MINUTES

WARM CARROT SALAD WITH ORANGE DRESSING

———————

- ⅓ cup (80ml) fresh orange juice
- 2 tbsp extra virgin olive oil
- ½ tsp honey
- ½ tsp white wine vinegar
- 1 tsp wholegrain mustard
- 3 medium carrots (360g), cut into 5mm (¼in) slices lengthways
- 1 small fennel (200g), cut into wedges
- ½ cup (50g) walnuts, toasted, chopped
- ½ cup flat-leaf parsley sprigs
- 150g (4½oz) ash goat's cheese

Heat a covered gas barbecue with all burners set to low and hood closed.

Whisk orange juice, oil, honey, vinegar and mustard in a small bowl until combined. Set aside.

Lift barbecue hood. Increase burners to high. Place carrot on the grill. Cook for 1 minute each side or until lightly charred. Remove. Repeat with fennel.

Place carrot, fennel, walnuts, parsley, and orange dressing in a large bowl; toss gently to combine. Season to taste.

Serve salad topped with chunks of goat's cheese.

SERVES *6*

PREP + COOK TIME 35 MINUTES

SINGAPORE CHILLI CRAB

————

1 live mud crab (2kg), killed humanely (see tips)

200g (6½oz) butter

6 cloves garlic, crushed

⅓ cup finely chopped coriander (cilantro) stems and roots

1½ tbsp grated fresh ginger

2 fresh long red chillies, seeds removed, chopped finely

2 tbsp freshly ground black pepper

½ tsp ground white pepper

6 green onions (scallions), sliced thinly

¼ cup (60ml) dark soy sauce

¼ cup (60ml) oyster sauce

1½ tbsp finely grated palm sugar

coriander (cilantro) leaves and extra sliced fresh red chilli, sliced lengthways, to serve

Heat a covered gas barbecue with all burners set to medium-high and hood closed.

Place crab on its back. Discard triangular flap at base of body. Pull away top shell. Remove grey gills and lungs found near lower legs. Using a large sharp knife, cut crab in half crossways. Using a meat mallet or crab cracker, lightly crack the shell of the legs and claws.

Cook crab on grill for 8 minutes on each side, with hood closed, until shells turn orange and meat is just cooked through. Remove from grill.

Meanwhile, heat a large wok over medium-high heat on barbecue's wok burner (see tips). Add butter; once melted, stir in garlic, coriander, ginger, chilli, peppers and half the green onion. Cook for 30 seconds. Stir in combined soy and oyster sauces with sugar. Bring to a gentle simmer. Cook for 1 minute or until thickened. Add crab to wok, tossing well to coat in sauce.

Serve crab topped with remaining green onion, coriander leaves and extra red chilli.

TIPS Ask your fish monger to prepare the crab for you. If you don't have a wok burner on your barbecue, you can use your regular stovetop, or a large frying pan instead of a wok.
You can serve crab with steamed jasmine rice, if you like.

SERVES *6*

PREP + COOK TIME 30 MINUTES (+ OVERNIGHT REFRIGERATION)

STICKY JERK PORK WITH CHARRED PINEAPPLE

---

3 pork tenderloins (1.2kg)

400g (12½oz) pineapple, peeled, cut into 1cm (½in) rounds

1 Lebanese cucumber (130g), chopped finely

2 eschalots (50g), chopped finely

1 fresh long green chilli, thinly sliced

2 tbsp lime juice

micro coriander (cilantro) leaves, to serve

JERK MARINADE

1 tsp ground allspice

1 tsp sweet paprika

1 tbsp thyme leaves

¼ cup (60ml) lime juice

2 cloves garlic

2 tbsp firmly packed brown sugar

1 fresh long green chilli, seeded, sliced thinly

1 tsp sea salt flakes

¼ cup (60ml) olive oil

You will need to start this recipe 1 day ahead.

Make jerk marinade.

Place pork in a deep tray; pour over jerk marinade. Cover; refrigerate overnight.

Bring pork to room temperature. Reserve remaining marinade. Meanwhile, heat a covered gas barbecue with all burners set to medium-high heat and hood closed.

Cook pork, turning occasionally for 12 minutes, brushing with reserved marinade, until dark golden and charred. Remove from heat; loosely cover with foil. Rest for 5 minutes.

Cook pineapple for 2 minutes each side or until tender and charred. Remove from heat; cut in half.

Combine cucumber, eschalots, chilli and lime juice in a bowl. Season to taste.

Thickly slice pork and thread onto skewers with charred pineapple. Serve pork and pineapple skewers with cucumber salsa and coriander.

JERK MARINADE Place ingredients in a small food processor or high-speed blender; process until smooth.

SERVES 4–6

PREP + COOK TIME 30 MINUTES

CHERMOULA–STUFFED SARDINES

¼ cup (40g) fine bulgur wheat

1½ tsp ground cumin

¼ cup finely chopped coriander (cilantro) leaves and stems

¼ cup finely chopped flat-leaf parsley

1 fresh long red chilli

2 cloves garlic

2 tsp finely grated lemon rind

1 tbsp extra virgin olive oil, plus extra for drizzling

18 whole sardines (1.5kg), cleaned

1 large lemon (200g), cut into 6 wedges

Heat a covered gas barbecue with all burners set to low and hood closed. (Alternatively, prepare a charcoal barbecue to low heat according to instructions on pages 10-11.)

Place bulgur and cumin in a medium heatproof bowl. Pour over ¼ cup (60ml) boiling water. Cover; stand for 10 minutes. Fluff with a fork. Cool to room temperature. Stir in coriander, parsley, chilli, garlic, lemon rind and oil. Season to taste.

Using a small knife, widen the slit along the sardine belly lengthways to run from head to tail. Using scissors, snip the backbone at the head and then again at the tail. Gently ease out the backbone and discard. Place sardines, skin-side down, on a clean work surface. Press 2 teaspoons of bulgur mixture down the centre of each sardine. Fold over to enclose.

Oil a fish grilling basket; place sardines in a single layer in basket. Cook on grill for 2 minutes each side or until just cooked through. Cook lemon wedges on grill for 1 minute each side or until charred and caramelised.

Squeeze the juice from 2 of the lemon wedges over the sardines, then drizzle with extra oil. Season to taste. Serve sardines with remaining charred lemon wedges.

TIP Sardines can be stuffed a day ahead. Store flat in an airtight container in the fridge with baking paper between layers.

SERVES 6

PREP + COOK TIME 45 MINUTES

PORK AND KIMCHI BURGERS

———————

800g (1½lb) minced (ground) pork

1½ cups (120g) thinly shredded wombok (napa cabbage)

4 green onions (scallions), chopped finely

2 tbsp Korean miso

1½ tbsp gochujang (Korean chilli paste)

1 tbsp dark soy sauce

2 tsp ground white pepper

2 tsp sesame oil

2 cups (400g) kimchi

1 small carrot (70g), halved, julienned

½ cup (150g) Kewpie (Japanese) mayonnaise

6 brioche burger buns (380g), split

1 cup coriander (cilantro) leaves

Heat a covered gas barbecue with all burners set to high and hood closed. (Alternatively, prepare a charcoal barbecue to medium heat according to instructions on pages 10-11.)

Place pork, wombok, green onion, 1 tablespoon of the miso, 1 tablespoon of the gochujang, the soy sauce, pepper and sesame oil in a large bowl. Mix with your hands to combine well. Season with salt. Divide mixture into 6 portions and shape into patties.

Drain kimchi, reserving 1 tablespoon of the liquid. Combine kimchi and carrot in a medium bowl. Combine reserved kimchi liquid and mayonnaise with the remaining miso and gochujang miso in a bowl.

Cook patties on grill for 5 minutes each side or until cooked through. Toast the buns, cut-side down, on grill for 30 seconds or until lightly charred.

Divide kimchi salad and coriander among bun bases, dollop with mayonnaise mixture, then top with pork patty. Top with the bun lid and serve.

SIDE SALADS

ROASTED CORN AND AVOCADO SALAD

PREP + COOK TIME 20 MINUTES (+ COOLING) **SERVES** 6

Cook 4 trimmed corn cobs (1kg) on a heated oiled grill or barbecue until charred. When cool enough to handle, cut kernels from cobs. Place kernels in a medium bowl with 1 thinly sliced small red onion, 2 thinly sliced large avocados (640g), 250g (8oz) halved cherry tomatoes, 2 tbsp lime juice and ¼ cup micro coriander (cilantro) leaves; toss gently to combine. Season to taste.

CRUNCHY PICKLED SALAD

PREP + COOK TIME 15 MINUTES (+ STANDING) **SERVES** 6

Thinly slice 1 small (100g) red onion. Combine ⅓ cup (80ml) white wine vinegar, 2 tbsp caster (superfine) sugar, 3 tsp dijon mustard and ¼ tsp chilli flakes in a large glass bowl; season. Add 4 chopped, seeded Lebanese cucumbers (520g), 250g (8oz) trimmed, thinly sliced radishes and sliced onions to dressing in bowl; toss to coat. Stand for 10 minutes. Add 1 thinly sliced fennel bulb (300g) to cucumber mixture in bowl; stir to combine. Season to taste. Transfer salad to a serving platter; top with ⅓ cup dill, ½ cup (50g) roasted walnuts and ½ cup (40g) shaved parmesan. Salad is best made just before serving.

SWEET PEPERONATA SALAD

PREP + COOK TIME 20 MINUTES (+ COOLING) **SERVES** 6

Thickly slice 6 mixed red, yellow and green capsicums (bell peppers) (1.2kg). Drizzle 1 tbsp extra virgin olive oil on a heated barbecue flat plate over medium-high heat. Cook capsicum, turning, for 8 minutes or until tender. Transfer to a large heatproof bowl; cool slightly. Add ¼ cup extra virgin olive oil, ¼ cup sherry vinegar, 2 tbsp honey, 1 finely chopped eschalot and 1 crushed clove garlic to capsicums in bowl; mix well to combine. Season to taste. Transfer salad to a large platter, top with parsley (or baby basil leaves) and baby capers.

SERVES 4

PREP + COOK TIME 25 MINUTES (+ REFRIGERATION)

LOBSTER TAILS WITH SMOKY CHILLI MAYO AND HERB OIL

8 uncooked lobster tails (1.8kg)

1¼ cups (310ml) extra virgin olive oil

3 cloves garlic, crushed, separated

1 tbsp finely grated lemon rind

½ tsp dried chilli flakes

2 fresh long red chillies

1 cup (230g) mayonnaise

1 tbsp lemon juice

1 tsp smoked paprika

HERB OIL

⅔ cup (160ml) extra virgin olive oil

1 cup flat-leaf parsley leaves, chopped finely

½ cup oregano leaves, chopped finely

1 tbsp finely grated lemon rind

1 tbsp lemon juice

1 tbsp sherry vinegar

Place lobster tails, soft-side up on a chopping board. Using scissors, cut slits along the belly where the grooves of the spine are. Turn the lobster tail over and cut down the spine without cutting all the way through the meat.

Combine 2 tablespoons of the oil, 2 of the garlic cloves, the lemon rind and chilli flakes in a large bowl. Add lobster tails and toss to coat. Cover; refrigerate for 1 hour.

Make herb oil.

Heat a covered gas barbecue with all burners set to high and hood closed.

Cook whole chillies on grill, turning, for 3 minutes or until charred. Remove from heat; cool. Peel away skin, remove seeds and finely chop flesh. Stir into mayonnaise with lemon juice, paprika, and remaining garlic. Season to taste.

Season lobster tails. Cook lobster on grill for 3 minutes each side or until charred and just cooked through.

Top lobster with herb oil and serve with smoky chilli mayo.

HERB OIL Place ingredients in a small food processor; process until coarsely chopped. Transfer to a small bowl; season to taste.

SERVES *6*

PREP + COOK TIME 1 HOUR

VEGETABLE BURGER WITH LIME GUACAMOLE

⅓ cup (80ml) extra virgin
   olive oil

1 tbsp white wine vinegar

1 tbsp dried oregano

2 cloves garlic, crushed

1 red capsicum (bell pepper)
   (200g), cut into wide strips

1 green capsicum (bell pepper)
   (200g), cut into wide strips

1 yellow capsicum (bell pepper)
   (200g), cut into wide strips

2 medium zucchini (240g),
   sliced thickly

1 medium eggplant (300g),
   cut into thick rounds

⅓ cup (80ml) extra virgin
   olive, extra

6 sesame brioche buns (380g),
   split

1 small red onion (100g),
   cut into thick rounds

1 cos (romaine) lettuce,
   shredded coarsely

hot sauce, to serve

LIME GUACAMOLE

2 medium avocados (500g)

2 limes (130g), rind finely
   grated, juiced

1 tbsp Kewpie (Japanese)
   mayonnaise

Heat a covered gas barbecue with all burners set to high and hood closed.

For the dressing, combine olive oil, vinegar, oregano and garlic in a large bowl. Set aside.

Place capsicums, zucchini, eggplant and extra olive oil in another large bowl. Season. Toss until well coated.

Reduce burners to medium. Cook vegetables on grill, for 3 minutes each side, or until crisp-tender. Transfer vegetables to dressing; toss to coat. Set aside.

Make lime guacamole.

Spread bun bases with guacamole. Top with grilled vegetables, onion and lettuce. Drizzle with hot sauce before capping with bun tops. Secure with a wooden skewer, if required.

LIME GUACAMOLE Place avocado flesh, lime rind and juice, and mayonnaise in a medium bowl. Crush with the back of a fork until a chunky paste forms. Season to taste.

SERVES *6*

PREP + COOK TIME 1 HOUR 15 MINUTES

LAMB-STUFFED EGGPLANT WITH LABNE DRESSING

- **3 small eggplants (690g), halved lengthways**
- **¼ cup (60ml) extra virgin olive oil**
- **1 tbsp ground cumin**
- **1 medium onion (150g), chopped finely**
- **2 cloves garlic, crushed**
- **½ tsp chilli flakes**
- **300g (9½oz) minced (ground) lamb**
- **2 medium tomatoes (300g), seeded, chopped**
- **1 tbsp tomato paste**
- **⅓ cup finely chopped flat-leaf parsley**
- **2 tbsp grape molasses (see tip)**
- **200g (6½oz) store-bought labne**
- **1 tsp grape molasses, extra**

Heat a covered gas barbecue with flat plate, with outside burners set to low and hood closed.

Using a sharp knife, score the flesh of the eggplant 1cm (½in) deep in a cross-hatch pattern. Brush flesh evenly with 2 tablespoons of the oil. Sprinkle with half the cumin; season.

Cook eggplant on flat plate, cut-side down for 5 minutes or until golden and tender. Remove from heat. Cool slightly. Combine remaining oil, cumin, the onion, garlic, chilli flakes and lamb. Cook mixture on flat plate, tossing continuously for 8 minutes or until cooked through.

Scoop the flesh out from the eggplant leaving a 1cm (½in) border. Chop flesh and combine with cooked lamb mixture, chopped tomato, tomato paste, ¼ cup of the parsley and the molasses in a large bowl.

Spoon filling evenly into eggplant halves. Place on barbecue flat plate. Cook, with hood closed for 10 minutes or until eggplant is cooked through.

Combine labne and extra molasses in a small bowl. Season to taste. Dollop spoonfuls on top of eggplant. Sprinkle with remaining parsley to serve.

TIP Grape molasses (Pekmez) is made from reduced grape must. it is available from specialist food stores. Substitute with pomegranate molasses, if preferred.

RECIPE PAGES 120–121

BBQ BRISKET

SERVES 8

PREP + COOK TIME 4 HOURS 45 MINUTES (+ HEATING & STANDING)

BBQ BRISKET

———

WHILE RELATIVELY NEW TO AUSTRALIAN PLATES, BRISKET IS A CELEBRATED PART OF AMERICAN-STYLE BARBECUING. A TOUGHER CUT, BRISKET BENEFITS FROM A LONG COOKING TIME, WHICH TRANSFORMS IT INTO A LUSCIOUS MELT-IN-YOUR-MOUTH TEXTURE.

4 quantities Cajun spice rub (see page 40)

½ cup (60g) sea salt flakes

2 tbsp extra virgin olive oil

5kg (10lb) piece lean beef brisket

4 eschalots (100g), skin-on, halved lengthways

1 head garlic, halved, broken into pieces

8 thyme sprigs

hot sauce, to serve

Combine Cajun spice rub and salt in a small bowl.

Heat a covered gas barbecue with all burners set to medium and hood closed, until temperature reaches 180°C/350°F on a thermometer. Place a large flameproof roasting pan inside barbecue to heat.

Rub oil over brisket; season. Sear brisket in heated roasting pan for 3 minutes each side or until lightly browned. Remove pan from heat; transfer brisket to a large plate or board, and when cool enough to handle, cover fat side with spice rub to coat evenly.

Place eschalots, garlic and thyme in roasting pan in a single layer and sit brisket on top. Pour 1½ cups (375ml) water into pan. Return pan to barbecue with hood closed and cook for 25 minutes. Turn middle burners off and outer burners to low heat, until temperature reaches 150°C/300°F on a thermometer. Cover brisket with a double layer of foil.

Cook brisket, adding more water to pan as necessary to prevent base from burning, for 3 hours and 50 minutes or until meat is very tender. Check meat at 3 hours 20 minutes.

Remove foil. Increase burners to high. Spoon pan juices over meat and cook for a further 20 minutes or until deep golden brown. Remove from heat. Rest for 15 minutes.

Slice brisket thickly; serve with hot sauce.

SERVING SUGGESTION
Serve with Crunchy Pickled Salad (see page 112).

PREP + COOK TIME 10 MINUTES (+ HEATING)

GRILLED SCALLOPS WITH CAFÉ DE PARIS BUTTER

———————

150g (4½oz) unsalted butter, softened

3 white anchovy fillets (10g), chopped finely

1 tbsp baby capers, chopped

1 clove garlic, crushed

1 tbsp chopped dill

2 tsp Worcestershire sauce

2 tsp tomato paste

24 scallops without roe on half shell (840g)

2 tbsp extra virgin olive oil

2 tsp finely grated lemon rind

micro herbs, to serve

Heat a covered gas barbecue with flat plate, with all burners set to medium and hood closed.

Stir butter, anchovies, capers, garlic, dill, Worcestershire sauce and tomato paste in a small bowl until very well combined. Season.

Brush scallops with combined olive oil and lemon rind. Season.

Cook scallops on barbecue flat plate, flesh-side down for 1 minute. Turn. Spoon butter mixture into scallops. Cook for a further 1 minute or until butter is melted and scallop is tender.

Sprinkle with micro herbs. Serve immediately.

MAKES 8

PREP + COOK TIME 35 MINUTES

TORNADO POTATOES WITH CHARRED GREEN ONION SOUR CREAM

2 tsp sweet paprika

2 tsp garlic powder

1 tsp onion powder

1 tsp chicken stock powder (see tip)

¼ tsp cayenne pepper

⅓ cup (80ml) extra virgin olive oil

8 small potatoes (960g), scrubbed

CHARRED GREEN ONION SOUR CREAM

6 green onions (scallions)

1 tbsp extra virgin olive oil

300g (9½oz) sour cream

2 tsp lemon juice

1 small clove garlic, crushed

Heat a covered gas barbecue with all burners set to low and hood closed.

Combine paprika, garlic, onion and stock powders, cayenne and oil in a small bowl. Season.

Thread potatoes onto metal skewers lengthways. Using a small sharp knife, make a small slice at the top of the potato, cutting until you hit the skewer. Keeping your knife in place, gradually twist the potato, cutting downwards to form a spiral. Gently pull cuts apart. Repeat with remaining potatoes.

Brush potatoes all over with spice mix. Wrap in foil. Cook on grill, with hood closed, for 15 minutes. Turn potatoes and cook for a further 15 minutes or until tender. Open foil and brush with any remaining spice mix. Close foil and cook for a further 5 minutes, turning, until lightly charred.

Meanwhile, make charred green onion sour cream.

Serve potatoes with green onion cream.

CHARRED GREEN ONION SOUR CREAM Coat green onions in oil. Cook on grill for 10 minutes or until charred. Set aside to cool completely. Coarsely chop green onion. Combine with remaining ingredients in a medium bowl. Season to taste.

TIP Replace chicken stock powder with vegetable stock powder for a vegetarian-friendly version.

MAKES *6*

PREP + COOK TIME 1 HOUR (+ HEATING)

BOLANI (STUFFED AFGHANI FLATBREAD)

---

3 cups (450g) plain (all-purpose) flour

½ teaspoon salt

¼ cup (60ml) extra virgin olive oil, plus extra to brush

2 large potatoes (600g), peeled, sliced thinly

8 green onions (scallions), sliced thinly

¾ cup thinly sliced garlic chives (see tip)

¾ cup finely chopped coriander (cilantro) leaves and stems

2 fresh long green chillies, chopped finely

1 tbsp finely grated lemon rind

2 tsp ground coriander

CUCUMBER YOGHURT

2 Lebanese cucumbers (260g)

1½ cups (420g) Greek yoghurt

1 small clove garlic, crushed

2 tsp dried mint

Combine flour and salt in a large bowl. Combine 1 tablespoon of the oil with 1¼ cups (310ml) warm water in a large jug. Gradually add liquid mixture to flour mixture and mix to form a soft dough. Turn dough onto a lightly floured surface. Knead for 3 minutes or until smooth. Cover; stand for 20 minutes.

Meanwhile, cook potatoes in boiling salted water for 8 minutes or until tender. Drain. Cool.

Combine potato, green onions, garlic chives, coriander, chilli, lemon rind and ground coriander with remaining oil in a large bowl, roughly breaking up the potato as you stir. Season to taste.

Heat a covered gas barbecue with all burners set to medium and hood closed. Meanwhile, make cucumber yoghurt.

Divide dough into 6 portions. Roll each portion into a ball. Working with one at a time, roll balls on a lightly floured surface into a 26cm (10in) round. Spread ¾ cup potato mixture over one half of dough, leaving a 2cm (¾in) border. Brush edge with water. Fold over and press down to seal.

Brush bolani with extra oil. Cook on grill for 3 minutes each side or until golden brown.

Serve bolani warm with cucumber yoghurt.

CUCUMBER YOGHURT Coarsely grate cucumbers. Place in a clean tea towel; squeeze over sink to remove excess moisture. Combine cucumber with remaining ingredients in a medium bowl. Season to taste.

TIP Garlic chives are available from Asian grocers and some greengrocers. They can be substituted with an equal quantity of green onions (scallions) plus 2 cloves crushed garlic.

SERVES *10*

PREP + COOK TIME 1 HOUR 30 MINUTES

BARBECUED MERINGUE WITH GINGER-SPICED STRAWBERRIES

6 egg whites

1½ cups (330g) caster (superfine) sugar

1 tsp apple cider vinegar

600ml thickened (heavy) cream

¼ cup (30g) flaked almonds, toasted

SPICED STRAWBERRIES

500g (1lb) strawberries, hulled

¼ cup (55g) caster (superfine) sugar

½ cup (140g) crystallised ginger, chopped coarsely

Heat a large covered gas barbecue with all burners set to medium-high heat and hood closed, until temperature reaches 180°C/350°F on a thermometer.

Line a large oven tray with baking paper. Trace a 26cm (10½in) circle on a second sheet of baking paper (see tips); place, marked-side down, on lined tray.

Whisk egg whites in a bowl of an electric mixer until soft peaks form. Add sugar, 1 tablespoon at a time, beating until sugar dissolves and meringue is thick and glossy. Whisk in vinegar until combined.

Spread meringue evenly inside the marked circle. Using the back of a spoon, create decorative swirls around the edge.

Place a trivet or upturned roasting tray on one side of barbecue. Place meringue tray over trivet. Turn off burners under meringue and reduce heat on the other side to medium. Close the hood. Cook for 1 hour, rotating tray halfway through cooking time, or until meringue is dry to the touch and slightly golden. Remove; cool completely on tray.

Make spiced strawberries.

Whisk cream in a clean bowl of an electric mixer until firm peaks form. Spoon cream over meringue; top with spiced strawberries and sauce. Scatter with almonds.

SPICED STRAWBERRIES Combine ingredients in a small saucepan. Place pan on barbecue, set to medium heat. Close the hood. Cook for 15 minutes, stirring occasionally, or until strawberries are soft and sauce is thick. Cool.

TIPS Lining the oven tray with two layers of baking paper will prevent the base of the meringue from overbrowning. Alternatively bake meringue in a 120°C/250°F fan-forced oven for 1 hour 20 minutes.

SERVES *6*

PREP + COOK TIME 25 MINUTES (+ REFRIGERATION)

GRILLED SUMMER FRUIT WITH SMOKED CINNAMON CUSTARD

———

1 tbsp finely grated orange rind

¼ cup (60ml) orange juice

2 tbsp brown sugar

3 medium yellow peaches (450g), stoned, quartered

6 purple figs (360g), halved

125g (4oz) strawberries, halved

2 tbsp melted butter

finely chopped pistachios, to serve

SMOKED CINNAMON CUSTARD

3 cinnamon sticks

2 cups (500ml) thickened (heavy) cream

¼ cup (55g) brown sugar

6 egg yolks

¼ cup (55g) caster (superfine) sugar

Heat a covered gas barbecue with all burners set to low and hood closed.

Meanwhile, make smoked cinnamon custard.

Combine orange rind and juice, and sugar in a medium bowl. Add peaches, figs and strawberries; toss gently to coat. Drizzle with melted butter.

Cook fruit on grill for 1 minute each side, brushing with any remaining orange mixture, until hot and grill marks appear.

To serve, spoon custard into serving glasses or bowls. Top with fruit and pistachios.

SMOKED CINNAMON CUSTARD Using tongs, carefully ignite cinnamon sticks over a direct flame until smoking. Place cinnamon sticks, cream and brown sugar in a medium saucepan over medium heat; bring to a gentle simmer. Remove pan from heat. Whisk egg yolks and caster sugar in a medium bowl until thick and pale. Gradually pour cream mixture into egg mixture, whisking continuously. Return mixture to pan over medium heat. Cook, stirring, for 5 minutes or until mixture thickens and coats the back of a spoon. Strain custard into a heatproof bowl; discard cinnamon sticks. Cover custard directly with plastic wrap. Refrigerate for 4 hours or until chilled.

SERVES *4*

PREP + COOK TIME 15 MINUTES (+ STANDING & FREEZING)

GRILLED PINEAPPLE AND LYCHEE SALAD WITH GINGER LIME GRANITA

500g (1lb) coconut yoghurt

140g (4½oz) coconut sugar

2 tsp vanilla bean paste

1 pineapple (900g), peeled, cut into eighths, cored

24 fresh lychees, peeled, pitted (scc tip)

micro mint, to serve

GINGER LIME GRANITA

½ cup (110g) caster (superfine) sugar

2 tsp finely grated fresh ginger

2 tsp finely grated lime rind

1½ tbsp lime juice

¾ cup (180ml) ginger beer

100ml soda water

Make ginger lime granita.

Heat a covered gas barbecue with all burners set to low and hood closed.

Combine coconut yoghurt, 85g (3oz) of the coconut sugar and the vanilla in a large bowl. Refrigerate until ready to serve.

Toss pineapple and remaining coconut sugar in a large bowl. Cook pineapple on grill for 2 minutes each side or until caramelised, warm and tender. Cool.

To serve, spoon yoghurt mixture into bowls. Top with pineapple and lychees. Scrape granita using a fork; spoon on top of fruit. Sprinkle with mint.

GINGER LIME GRANITA Place sugar, ginger, lime rind and 225ml water in a small saucepan over medium heat; stir until sugar dissolves. Remove from heat. Stand for 30 minutes to infuse. Stir in lime juice. Strain syrup into a 18cm x 26cm (7¼in x 10½in) slice pan. Stir in ginger beer and soda water. Cover with foil; freeze for 3 hours or until almost set. Using a fork, scrape the granita from bottom and sides of pan, combining frozen mixture with unfrozen mixture. Cover and return to the freezer until frozen.

TIP You can use drained canned lychees instead of fresh lychees, if preferred.

SMOKE

THE PROCESS OF SMOKING, ADDING WOOD CHIPS
OR OTHER AROMATS TO A FIRE OR BARBECUE, IS
NOT A COOKING METHOD AS SUCH, BUT A WAY TO
IMBUE YOUR FOOD WITH THE RICH AND EARTHY
COMPLEXITY THAT SMOKE BRINGS TO A DISH.

SMOKING GUIDE

Smoking adds a rich layer of flavour, increasing the umami effect, which make foods more savoury. Smoke is made of many things, some of which inhibit the growth of microbes, and others that retard oxidisation of fat. This is what makes it a preservative, in combination with salt.

SMOKING (BARBECUING)

COLD AND HOT SMOKING

Cold smoking is done at temperatures no higher than 29°C (85°F), which doesn't actually cook food; however, it is usually salted/cured first. Hot smoking, actually cooks food. Fish is generally smoked between 82°C and 93°C (180°F-200°F) and meat 115°C (240°F). In the cold-smoking process, food is placed far from the heat source so it smokes long and slow. Conversely, with hot smoking, the smoke source is positioned closer to the food.

Salting Salting is the first step in cold smoking. Its purpose is two fold: to partially dry the food and hence remove some of the moisture that microbes might be attracted to, and to season. Even for cold smoking where temperatures are low, this first process of salting, will change the texture of the meat or fish, making it firmer. The quantity of dry salt or the concentration of salt in the brine required is higher for cold smoking. After salting, food is briefly rinsed and allowed to dry before smoking.

SMOKING CHIPS AND WOOD

Hard woods such as hickory, oak, maple and mesquite are all good choices. Wood chips, available from barbecue shops, must be soaked first in cold water so they smoulder slowly over the fire, rather than burn. For additional flavours, soak a variety of herbs and spices in the water with the wood chips.

To ensure that the wood hasn't been treated with chemicals, it is best to buy woods specifically sold for smoking (usually found in barbecue shops). You can also use herbs or, for tea smoking, a combination of tea leaves, brown sugar and rice. You can use a smoker box to hold the wood chips and follow your barbecue instructions. The food to be smoked is added once the chips start to smoke, either directly on the grill grates or in a separate container, and is cooked with the hood closed. For charcoal barbecues, lumps of smoking wood are added directly to the coals.

WOK SMOKER

An old wok works well as an improvised smoker. Line the wok with foil, place the wood chips on the base, with a rack or trivet in the base to elevate the food. Place the food on top of rack, ensuring there's space in between for the smoke to circulate. Cover with a tight-fitting lid and put the extractor fan on, if you are inside. Once smoke is produced, you can reduce the heat to low for the rest of the cooking time.

01

02

03

01 Charcoal smoker There are many smokers and cross-purpose barbecues on the market. Pick the best one for your space, budget and skill level.

02 Wok method Line an old wok with foil and place wood chips in the centre. Set a rack or trivet over the chips and when smoking, cover with a tight-fitting lid.

03 Smoker box Barbecue smoker boxes are filled with wood chips, which, when placed over a charcoal or gas flame produce smoke in the barbecue.

SERVES 4

PREP + COOK TIME 3 HOURS 30 MINUTES (+ OVERNIGHT REFRIGERATION, HEATING & STANDING)

TEXAN SMOKED RIBS

3kg (6lb) American-style
  pork ribs (see tip)
2 tbsp sweet paprika
1 tbsp ground cumin
1 tsp cayenne pepper
1 tsp onion powder
1 tsp garlic powder
1 tbsp sea salt flakes
1 tbsp brown sugar
2 cups (225g) hickory
  wood chips
4 trimmed corn cobs (1kg)

BARBECUE SAUCE
2 cups (500ml) barbecue sauce
½ cup (125ml) beer
½ cup (125ml) maple syrup
¼ cup (60ml) apple cider vinegar

You will need to start this recipe 1 day ahead.

Using a small knife, trim membrane from the back of the ribs. Place ribs on a tray. Combine spices, onion and garlic powders, salt and sugar in a small bowl. Rub spice mixture over the top of the ribs. Refrigerate, covered, overnight.

Soak half the wood chips in a small bowl of water for 30 minutes; drain. Heat a large covered gas barbecue with all burners set to medium-high heat and hood closed, until temperature reaches 180°C/350°F on a thermometer.

Combine soaked and remaining dry wood chips in a barbecue smoker box. Place box in barbecue and close hood; leave for 10 minutes or until chips begin to smoke.

Meanwhile, make barbecue sauce. Reserve ¾ cup of the sauce for serving.

Brush ribs with a little of the remaining sauce; place on a barbecue rack overhanging the smoke box in the barbecue. (Alternatively place over a wire rack on the grill side plate for indirect heat.) Cook ribs for 3 hours, brushing with remaining sauce every 15 minutes or until ribs are tender and darkly glazed.

Meanwhile, when ribs are almost cooked, place corn directly on the grill; cook, turning occasionally, for 10 minutes or until charred. Cut into smaller pieces.

Cut ribs into short lengths and serve with reserved warmed sauce and corn cobs.

BARBECUE SAUCE Bring ingredients to the boil in a medium saucepan over high heat. Reduce heat; simmer for 8 minutes or until reduced and sauce thickens slightly.

TIP American-style pork ribs are also known as baby back ribs; they are cut from the top of the rib cage, are slightly curved, taper in size and carry more meat on and between the ribs than spare ribs. Usually the ribs are sold in racks of between 10 and 13 ribs.

SERVES 4

PREP + COOK TIME 50 MINUTES (+ HEATING)

THE BIG SMOKE UP

---

2 cups (225g) hickory wood chips

1 bunch rosemary

8 small portobello mushrooms (400g)

200g (6½oz) cherry truss tomatoes

100g (3oz) butter, softened

1 tsp finely grated lemon rind

1 tbsp lemon thyme leaves, chopped finely

¼ cup flat-leaf parsley, chopped finely

1 clove garlic, crushed

1 tbsp vegetable oil, to brush

4 eggs

12 slices pancetta (180g)

8 slices sourdough bread (400g)

Heat covered gas barbecue with flat plat, with all burners set to high and hood closed. Soak half the wood chips and the rosemary for 30 minutes; drain.

Combine soaked wood chips and rosemary with remaining dry wood chips in a barbecue smoker box. Place box in barbecue and close lid; leave to heat for 10 minutes or until mixture begins to smoke.

Place mushrooms and tomatoes on barbecue's hanging rack. Close hood; smoke for 30 minutes.

Meanwhile, mix butter, lemon rind, thyme, parsley and garlic in a small bowl. Season. Spread butter evenly over mushrooms. Close hood. Cook for a further 2 minutes or until butter begins to melt. Remove mushrooms and tomatoes. Remove smoker box.

Brush barbecue flat plate with oil. Fry eggs on flat plate for 3 minutes, or until whites are set, edges are crisp and yolks are cooked to your liking. Cook pancetta for 2 minutes each side or until crisp. Toast bread for 2 minutes each side or until golden.

Serve mushrooms, tomatoes, eggs, pancetta and toast on a large serving platter.

SERVES 4

PREP + COOK TIME 45 MINUTES (+ HEATING)

SMOKY EGGPLANT SALAD WITH CHARRED CHILLI DRESSING

2 tbsp grapeseed oil

2 tbsp sesame oil

2 tbsp light soy sauce

1 tbsp finely grated fresh ginger

1 clove garlic, grated finely

2 large eggplants (1kg), cut into 1cm (½in) slices lengthways

4 Japanese eggplants (360g), halved lengthways

250g (8oz) mixed cherry tomatoes, halved

300g (9½oz) firm tofu, torn into 1cm (½in) pieces

2 green onions (scallions), sliced thinly

1 cup coriander (cilantro) leaves

toasted sesame seeds, to serve

CHARRED CHILLI DRESSING

2 fresh long red chilies

3 green onions (scallions), sliced thinly

1½ tbsp finely grated ginger

1 small clove garlic, grated finely

½ cup (125ml) grapeseed oil

½ cup (125ml) light soy sauce

1½ tbsp black vinegar

3 tsp honey

3 tsp sesame oil

Prepare a charcoal barbecue on medium heat according to instructions on pages 10-11.

Make charred chilli dressing.

Combine oils, soy sauce, ginger and garlic in a small bowl. Brush mixture all over eggplants. Cook eggplants over hot coals, turning occasionally, for 12 minutes or until tender.

To serve, top eggplant with tomatoes, tofu, green onion and coriander. Drizzle with dressing and sprinkle with sesame seeds.

CHARRED CHILLI DRESSING Place chillies directly on hot coals. Cook, turning occasionally, for 10 minutes or until blackened and blistered. Transfer to a heatproof bowl and cover; stand for 15 minutes. Peel away charred skin and finely chop flesh. Place chilli, green onion, ginger and garlic in a small heatproof bowl. Heat grapeseed oil in small saucepan over high heat until almost smoking. Carefully pour hot oil over chilli mixture; stir to combine. Set aside for 5 minutes to infuse. Stir in soy sauce, vinegar, honey and sesame oil. Season with pepper.

SERVES *4*

PREP + COOK TIME 1 HOUR 25 MINUTES (+ OVERNIGHT REFRIGERATION + HEATING)

HOT WINGS WITH SMOKY CHEDDAR DIPPING SAUCE

⅓ cup (95g) tomato sauce (ketchup)

1 tsp garlic powder

⅓ cup (80ml) maple syrup

2 tsp English mustard

¼ cup (60ml) hot sauce

1.5 kg (3lb) chicken wings, trimmed

2 cups (225g) hickory wood chips

SMOKY CHEDDAR DIPPING SAUCE

20g (¾oz) butter

1 tbsp plain (all-purpose) flour

½ cup (125ml) milk

1 tsp English mustard

¾ cup (90g) grated smoked cheddar

½ cup (120g) sour cream

You will need to start this recipe 1 day ahead.

Combine tomato sauce, garlic powder, maple syrup, mustard and hot sauce in a small bowl.

Place chicken wings in a large bowl; add ¼ cup of the sauce mixture and stir to coat. Refrigerate, covered, overnight.

Heat a covered gas barbecue with all burners set to low and hood closed. Soak half the wood chips; drain. Combine soaked wood chips and the remaining dry wood chips in a barbecue smoking box. Place box in barbecue and close lid; leave to heat for 10 minutes or until mixture begins to smoke.

Meanwhile, line a large oven tray with foil. Place wings in a single layer on tray. Place tray on grill away from direct heat. Cook, with hood closed, for 45 minutes or until just tender.

Remove tray and smoke box from barbecue. Increase heat to high. Cook wings directly on grill, turning occasionally for 4 minutes or until charred and cooked.

Meanwhile, place remaining sauce in a small saucepan over medium heat. Bring to a gentle simmer. Set aside.

Make smoky cheddar dipping sauce.

Toss wings in warmed sauce. Serve wings with dipping sauce. Sprinkle with freshly ground black pepper, if you like.

SMOKY CHEDDAR DIPPING SAUCE Melt butter in a small saucepan over low-medium heat. Whisk in flour until combined. Gradually add milk, whisking continuously until thickened. Stir in mustard, cheddar and sour cream until smooth and melted. Remove from heat. Cover surface directly with baking paper. Keep warm.

TIP If smoky cheddar sauce gets too cold and thick, return to a medium-low heat with 1 tablespoon milk and stir until warm.

SERVES 4

PREP + COOK TIME 30 MINUTES (+ HEATING)

HOT–SMOKED SNAPPER WITH BACON AND CORN SALSA

½ cup (100g) white long-grain rice

¼ cup (55g) brown sugar

2 cups (140g) apple wood chips

4 x 200g boneless snapper fillets (800g), skin-on

1 tbsp extra virgin olive oil

BACON AND CORN SALSA

1 tbsp extra virgin olive oil

200g (6½oz) streaky bacon, sliced thinly

3 corn cobs (750g), kernels removed

2 green onions (scallions), sliced thinly

2 tbsp finely chopped flat-leaf parsley

2 tbsp white balsamic vinegar

Heat a covered gas barbecue with all burners set to medium and hood closed.

Combine rice, sugar and wood chips in a barbecue smoking box. Place box in barbecue and close lid; leave to heat for 10 minutes or until mixture begins to smoke.

Lightly oil a fish grilling basket. Brush snapper fillets with oil. Season. Place fillets in basket. Place basket, with fish skin-side up, on grill away from direct heat. Cook, with hood closed, for 4 minutes each side or until cooked through.

Meanwhile, make bacon and corn salsa.

Serve snapper with salsa.

BACON AND CORN SALSA Heat oil in a large non-stick frying pan over medium-high heat. Cook bacon for 6 minutes, stirring occasionally, or until crisp and fat has rendered. Stir in corn kernels; cook for 3 minutes or until corn is just tender. Transfer mixture to a large bowl with green onions, parsley and vinegar. Toss to combine. Season to taste.

TIPS This recipe doesn't require a smoker or barbecue, so you can use your stovetop, if preferred. Make sure to smoke in a very well ventilated area.

SERVES 6

PREP + COOK TIME 1 HOUR 15 MINUTES (+ OVERNIGHT REFRIGERATION & STANDING)

SMOKED PORK LOIN AND ROASTED GRAPES

½ cup (125ml) extra virgin olive oil

4 cloves garlic, crushed

1 tbsp finely grated orange rind

1 tbsp finely chopped rosemary

1.2kg (2½lb) rolled pork loin, skin scored

500g (1lb) smoking wood chips

1 tbsp fine sea salt

⅓ cup (80ml) orange juice

2 tbsp sherry vinegar

1½ tsp dark brown sugar

500g (1lb) seedless red grapes

TAHINI SAUCE

⅓ cup (90g) tahini

2 tbsp extra virgin olive oil

2 tsp lemon rind

1 tbsp lemon juice

1 tbsp sherry vinegar

½ small clove garlic, crushed

You will need to start this recipe 1 day ahead.

Combine oil, garlic, orange rind and chopped rosemary in a small bowl. Untie pork; brush mixture all over inside of pork. Re-roll pork and tie with kitchen string at 4cm (1½in) intervals. Cover; refrigerate for 6 hours or overnight.

Bring pork to room temperature. Place smoking chips in a large bowl of water; soak for 30 minutes. Drain.

Meanwhile, prepare a charcoal barbecue with hood to high heat according to instructions on pages 10-11. Temperature should read 220°C/425°F on a themometer.

Make tahini sauce.

Position coals to one side or barbecue; sprinkle half the smoking chips on the hot coals. Allow to burn and smoke. Rub pork with salt, place in a cast-iron roasting pan and sit pork on grill opposite to coals. Sprinkle remaining chips over the coals. Cook, hood closed, for 40 minutes or until pork reaches an internal temperature of 60°C. Remove pan from heat; rest pork for 30 minutes. Cut into thick slices.

Meanwhile, combine orange juice, vinegar and sugar in a bowl; add grapes and turn to coat. Six minues before pork is cooked, add grapes to the roasting pan, or on a shelf over the pork; cook, hood closed, over indirect heat for 6 minutes or until tender.

To serve, spoon tahini sauce onto plates. Top with sliced pork and roasted grapes. Spoon over pan juices.

TAHINI SAUCE Combine ingredients in a small bowl; whisk until smooth. Thin with a little water if necessary. Season to taste. Refrigerate until ready to serve.

BUTTERS
& SAUCES

JALAPEÑO KETCHUP SAUCE

PREP + COOK TIME 45 MINUTES (+ HEATING & COOLING)
MAKES 5 CUPS

Heat a gas barbecue flat plate to medium-high heat. Place 1.5kg seeded, quartered roma (plum) tomatoes, 2 large (400g) chopped onions, 6 cloves garlic, 2 chopped fresh jalapeño chillies, 2 tsp cumin seeds and 2 tbsp olive oil in a large bowl; toss to combine. Cook mixture on flat plate, turning, for 20 minutes or until softened. Transfer to a food processor; process tomato mixture, in batches, until smooth. Pour mixture in a large heavy-based saucepan with ½ cup (125ml) red wine vinegar, ¾ cup firmly packed brown sugar and 1 tbsp salt flakes; bring to a simmer over medium heat. Simmer for 30 minutes or until sauce has reduced and thickened. Season to taste. Cool to room temperature.

GOES WITH Barbecued beef or chicken burgers and fries.

TIP Store ketchup in sterilised jars or bottles in the fridge for up to 3 months.

NAM JIM BUTTER

PREP + COOK TIME 10 MINUTES **MAKES** ⅔ CUP

Place 200g (6oz) softened butter, 2 crushed cloves garlic, 1 seeded and chopped fresh green chilli, 2 tbsp finely chopped coriander (cilantro) root and 1 finely chopped eschalot in a bowl. Combine 2 tsp finely grated palm sugar, 1 tsp lime juice and 1 tsp fish sauce in a separate bowl, mix well until sugar dissolves. Add to butter mixture, mix until well combined; season with freshly ground pepper. Shape into a log; wrap in baking paper or plastic wrap. Refrigerate until required.

GOES WITH Barbecued or grilled meat, chicken or seafood.

TIP Freeze butter up to 3 months. Thaw in the fridge; stand for 30 minutes at room temperature before use.

ANCHOVY, PARSLEY AND GARLIC LEMON BUTTER

PREP + COOK TIME 10 MINUTES **MAKES** ⅔ CUP

Combine 200g (6oz) softened butter, 2 crushed cloves garlic, 2 tsp finely grated lemon rind, 3 finely chopped anchovy fillets and 1 tbsp finely chopped flat-leaf parsley in a bowl. Season with freshly ground pepper. Shape into a log; wrap in baking paper or plastic wrap. Refrigerate until required.

GOES WITH Barbecued steak, chicken or fish.

TIP Freeze butter up to 3 months. Thaw in the fridge; stand for 30 minutes at room temperature before use.

SERVES 4

PREP + COOK TIME 45 MINUTES (+ SOAKING & HEATING)

CEDAR-SMOKED RAINBOW TROUT

1 cedar smoking plank (see tips)

2 small ruby grapefruit (700g)

2 x 500g (1lb) whole rainbow trout, cleaned

1 bunch thyme

1 tbsp extra virgin olive oil

1 large avocado (320g), cut into thin wedges

4 cups (120g) picked watercress

finely grated fresh horseradish, to serve

HORSERADISH BUTTERMILK DRESSING

½ cup (125ml) buttermilk

2 tbsp extra virgin olive oil

2 tbsp whole-egg mayonnaise

1 tbsp finely grated fresh horseradish (see tips)

2 tsp apple cider vinegar

Soak cedar plank in cold water for 2 hours; drain.

Heat a covered gas barbecue with all burners set to medium-high and hood closed, until temperature reaches 200°C/400°F on a thermometer.

Finely grate rind from 1 grapefruit; reserve. Peel and segment both grapefruit over a bowl, squeezing the membrane to release the juice. Reserve 2 tablespoons juice for the dressing.

Make horseradish buttermilk dressing.

Fill trout cavities evenly with thyme, drizzle with oil; season. Place trout on plank, then place plank on the grill. Cook, hood closed, for 7 minutes. Turn trout over and cook, hood closed, for another 7 minutes or until cooked through. (Spritz plank with water during cooking if it is looking a bit dry.)

Meanwhile, combine grapefruit segments, avocado and watercress in a large bowl. Add half the dressing; toss to combine.

Peel back skin from trout. Arrange trout on a serving board; drizzle with remaining dressing. Serve with grapefruit salad topped with freshly grated horseradish.

HORSERADISH BUTTERMILK DRESSING Place ingredients in a screw-top jar with reserved grapefruit rind and juice; shake well to combine. Season to taste. Refrigerate until ready to serve.

TIPS Cedar grilling and smoking planks are available from barbecue supply and hardware stores. They impart a sweet, smoky robust flavour to foods and may be reused. You can swap fresh horseradish with prepared horseradish which is available from supermarkets and grocers.

SMOKED TOMATO
AND GARLIC TART
WITH CHILLI–
CHEESE PASTRY

SERVES *4*

PREP + COOK TIME 1 HOUR 45 MINUTES (+ HEATING)

SMOKED TOMATO AND GARLIC TART WITH CHILLI-CHEESE PASTRY

THIS RECIPE WOULD BE GREAT TO MAKE AT THE
HEIGHT OF TOMATO SEASON, USING ALL THE
DIFFERENT TYPES AND COLOURS OF TOMATOES
AVAILABLE. SERVE TART WITH A LEAFY GREEN SALAD,
DRESSED WITH BALSAMIC VINEGER AND OLIVE OIL.

2 cups (225g) hickory
    wood chips

1 cup (200g) white
    long-grain rice

4 cloves garlic

6 medium ripe tomatoes
    (900g), sliced thickly
    (see tips)

220g (7oz) firm ricotta

1 egg

¼ cup flat-leaf parsley leaves,
    chopped finely

1 tbsp chopped oregano

60g (2oz) baby rocket
    (arugula) leaves

**SMOKY CHILLI-
CHEESE PASTRY**

150g (4½oz) butter, chopped

2½ cups (375g) plain
    (all-purpose) flour

½ tsp sea salt flakes

1 tsp smoked paprika

½ tsp dried chilli flakes

¼ cup (30g) grated smoked
    cheddar

Heat a covered gas barbecue with all burners set to high and hood closed. Soak half the wood chips for 30 minutes; drain. Set aside.

Line a large flameproof roasting pan with foil. Place soaked chips and remaining dry wood chips with rice in pan and set a greased wire rack over wood mixture. Place pan in barbecue and close lid; leave to heat for 10 minutes or until mixture begins to smoke.

Wrap garlic cloves loosely in foil. Season tomatoes. Place garlic and tomatoes on wire rack. Cover with foil. Close hood. Turn off heat. Leave to smoke for 20 minutes. Remove garlic and tomatoes; cool to room temperature.

Meanwhile, make smoky chilli-cheese pastry. Heat barbecue with burners set to high and hood closed, until temperature reaches 220°C/425°F on a thermometer.

Mash smoked garlic with a fork in a bowl. Add ricotta, egg and herbs; mix until combined. Spoon mixture into the centre of the pastry leaving a 6cm (2½in) border. Top with tomatoes. Fold pastry edge inwards over filling, pressing to seal. Season with freshly ground black pepper.

Place tray with tart on a wire rack on the flat plate of the barbecue. Reduce burners to low. Cook, with hood closed for 45 minutes or until pastry is golden and cooked through.

Serve tart at room temperature topped with rocket.

SMOKY CHILLI–CHEESE PASTRY Place butter and ⅔ cup (160ml) water in a medium saucepan over high heat; bring to the boil. Remove from heat. Stir in flour, salt, paprika and chilli flakes. Fold in cheddar. Turn dough out onto a clean surface and knead until smooth. Roll dough out on a sheet of baking paper into a 40cm (16in) round. Transfer on paper to an oven tray.

TIPS Use a variety of tomatoes such as roma (plum), oxheart and vine-ripened. You can prepare this recipe over a gas or charcoal barbecue, or on a stovetop in a very well ventilated area.

SERVES 4

PREP + COOK TIME 50 MINUTES

LEMON MYRTLE-INFUSED LAMB BACKSTRAP

125g (4oz) butter, softened

2¾ tbsp ground lemon myrtle

1 clove garlic, crushed

3 tsp horseradish cream

50g (1½oz) applewood smoking chips

4 long large sprigs rosemary

4 x 180g (5½oz) lamb backstraps

1 tbsp sea salt flakes

1 tbsp extra virgin olive oil

Combine butter, 2 teaspoons of the lemon myrtle, the garlic and horseradish in a bowl. Shape into a log; wrap firmly in baking paper. Refrigerate until ready to serve.

Heat a covered gas barbecue with flat plate, with all burners set to high and hood closed. Soak wood chips for 30 minutes; drain. Set aside.

Fill a smoking box with soaked wood chips and 2 tablespoons lemon myrtle. Place smoking box directly on flat plate over burner. Close hood and leave to heat for 10 minutes or until mixture begins to smoke.

Meanwhile, remove two thirds of the leaves from each rosemary sprig; trim ends to form a point. Thread a lamb backstrap onto each sprig. Combine remaining 1 teaspoon lemon myrtle and the salt in a bowl. Brush lamb lightly with oil; sprinkle evenly with salt mixture.

Cook lamb on flat plat on the opposite side from smoke box for 4 minutes each side with hood closed for medium or until cooked to your liking. Remove; stand for 5 minutes.

Cut butter into slices and place on top of hot lamb. Cut lamb into thick slices to serve.

SERVES 4

PREP + COOK TIME 1 HOUR 30 MINUTES (+ REFRIGERATION)

SMOKED JASMINE TEA MACKEREL WITH DAIKON REMOULADE

---

4 whole mackerel
   (1.3kg), cleaned

½ cup (150g) rock salt

¼ cup (55g) demerara
   sugar

½ cup (100g) jasmine
   rice

½ cup (40g) loose leaf
   organic green tea

300g (9½oz) daikon,
   peeled

½ cup (125ml) store-
   bought roasted
   sesame dressing

1 tbsp dashi miso
   paste

1 tbsp lime juice

6 green onions
   (scallions),
   shredded, plus
   extra, to serve

50g (1½oz) Japanese
   pickled radish
   (takuan), chopped
   finely (see tip)

4 radishes (140g), cut
   into julienne

¼ cup (30g) furikake
   (seasoned seaweed
   flakes)

Pat mackerel dry with paper towel and place on a large oven tray. Combine salt and sugar in a small bowl. Sprinkle salt mixture in cavity of fish and over skin. Refrigerate for 45 minutes. Rinse off salt mixture with cold water. Pat dry with paper towel.

Meanwhile, place rice and tea leaves in a smoker box. Heat a covered gas barbecue with all burners set to high and hood closed. Sit smoker box on grill directly over burner. Close lid. When beginning to smoke, turn burners down to low.

Place mackerel in a single layer on a rack set over a foil tray. Fill the tray halfway with water. Place tray on the opposite side of the smoke box. Close hood. Smoke for 50 minutes or until fish flesh flakes easily.

Meanwhile, to make daikon remoulade, shred daikon finely using a julienne peeler or mandoline. Transfer to a large bowl with sesame dressing, miso, lime juice, green onion, pickled and red radishes.

Serve mackerel with daikon remoulade. Sprinkle with furikake and extra green onion.

TIP Japanese pickled radish (takuan) is available from Asian supermarkets. It is daikon radish and is yellow in colour.

MAKES 2 CUPS

PREP + COOK TIME 25 MINUTES

HERB—SMOKED OLIVES

10g (½oz) thyme sprigs, plus extra to serve
10g (½oz) rosemary leaves
10g (½oz) bay leaves
1 medium lemon (140g)
2 cups (320g) pitted mixed olives, drained
1 fresh long red chilli, sliced thinly
⅓ cup (80ml) extra virgin olive oil

Line the base of a heavy-based saucepan or wok with two layers of foil. Place thyme, rosemary and bay leaves in pan. Top with a small wire rack.

Using a vegetable peeler, peel lemon rind into strips. Place rind, olives, chilli and oil in a shallow heatproof dish. Place dish in pan on top of wire rack. Cover pan tightly with foil or lid.

Place pan over medium-high heat for 15 minutes. Remove from heat. Stand for 5 minutes before removing foil or lid.

Smoked olives can be served warm or at room temperature. Sprinkle with extra thyme sprigs. Store any remaining olives in an airtight container in the fridge for up to 2 weeks.

TIPS Smoked olives make a great addition to cocktails. Reserve smoked oil and use to drizzle over meats and vegetables, or in salad dressings.

RECIPE PAGES 172–173

SICHUAN–STYLE
SMOKED DUCK

PREP + COOK TIME 2 HOURS (+ OVERNIGHT REFRIGERATION & STANDING)

SICHUAN–STYLE SMOKED DUCK

———————

DUCK IS A GREAT PROTEIN TO SMOKE AS THEIR THICK LAYER OF FAT HELPS ABSORB THE SMOKE FLAVOUR, WHILE ALSO KEEPING THE DUCK MOIST. CHINESE PANCAKES, ALSO CALLED PEKING DUCK WRAPPERS, CAN BE FOUND IN SOME SUPERMARKETS AND ASIAN GROCERS. THIS RECIPE IS SMOKED USING THE STOVE.

YOU WILL NEED TO START THIS RECIPE 1 DAY AHEAD.

1 tbsp Sichuan peppercorns

1 tbsp black peppercorns

⅓ cup (40g) sea salt flakes

1 whole duck (2kg)

70g (2½oz) fresh ginger, sliced thickly

6 green onions (scallions), plus extra to serve

½ cup (40g) black tea leaves

½ cup (100g) jasmine rice

½ cup (110g) firmly packed brown sugar

1 medium mandarin (200g), rind peeled using a vegetable peeler

3 star anise

1 cinnamon stick

vegetable oil, for deep-frying

24 Chinese pancakes (360g), warmed

hoisin sauce and sliced cucumber, to serve

Heat a large wok over medium-high heat. Add Sichuan pepper, black pepper and salt; toast for 1 minute or until fragrant. Transfer to a spice grinder, high-speed blender or small food processor and process to form a fine powder. Rub mixture all over and inside duck. Place duck on a large tray. Refrigerate, uncovered, overnight.

Place duck in a colander in the sink. Boil a full kettle of water. Pour half the water over the skin. Carefully turn duck over and pour over remaining water. Place duck on a wire rack set over a large tray. Stand, uncovered, for 3 hours for skin to dry.

Fill duck cavity with ginger and green onion.

Line a large wok with foil. Combine tea, rice, sugar, mandarin rind, star anise and cinnamon in wok. Place a wire rack on top. Sit duck, breast-side up, on rack. Cover wok tightly with foil. Set wok over medium-high heat for 30 minutes or until duck is light brown. Transfer to a plate. Discard foil and smoking ingredients.

Return wok to medium-high heat. Pour 1 litre (4 cups) water into wok. Set same wire rack on top. Bring to the boil, then reduce heat to a gentle simmer. Sit duck, breast-side up on rack. Cover tightly with foil. Steam for 50 minutes, topping up water in wok if required, until cooked through.

Carefully transfer duck to a wire rack; cool for 30 minutes. Remove ginger and green onion. Drain any juices from centre of the duck. Pat dry with paper towel.

Fill cleaned and dried wok one-third full with oil. Place wok on medium heat and heat until oil reaches 180°C/350°F on a thermometer. Carefully lower duck, breast-side down into oil. If the duck is not fully submerged, ladle hot oil over any exposed skin. Cook for 6 minutes on each side or until crisp and golden. Drain on paper towel. Rest duck for 10 minutes.

Serve duck, sliced, in pancakes with hoisin sauce, cucumber and extra green onion.

DO AHEAD Scald and smoke the duck in the morning, then steam and fry close to serving. Drying the duck helps to crisp the skin but if you are short on time smoke duck after scalding.

SERVES 4

PREP + COOK TIME 40 MINUTES (+ SOAKING)

SMOKED SAUSAGE ROTI WRAP

1½ cups (170g) smoking wood chips

8 pork sausages (960g)

1 tbsp olive oil

4 eggs

4 store-bought roti (240g)

2 cups (40g) mixed salad leaves

2 tbsp chilli jam

coriander (cilantro) leaves, to serve

MINT RAITA

½ tsp cumin seeds

1 cup (280g) store-brought labne

⅓ cup (15g) finely chopped mint leaves

2 tsp lemon juice

1 small clove garlic, crushed

Cover wood chips in cold water; soak for 30 minutes.

Place soaked wood chips in a smoking box. Place box in a covered gas barbecue with all burners set to high and hood closed for 30 minutes or until smoking.

Cook sausages on grill, with hood closed, for 5 minutes each side or until cooked through.

Meanwhile, make mint raita.

Brush barbecue flat plate with oil. Fry eggs for 3 minutes, or until whites are set, edges are crisp and yolks are cooked to your liking. Heat roti on grill for 1 minute each side.

Cut sausages in half lengthways. Spread roti with 2 tablespoons mint raita and top with salad leaves, sausages and fried egg. Drizzle with chilli jam and scatter with coriander to serve. Fold over to enclose.

MINT RAITA Heat a small frying pan over medium-high heat. Toast cumin seeds for 1 minute or until fragrant. Combine cumin seeds, labne, mint, lemon juice and garlic in a medium bowl. Season to taste.

SERVES 4

PREP + COOK TIME 45 MINUTES (+ OVERNIGHT REFRIGERATION & HEATING)

ROASTED PLUMS AND BLACKBERRIES WITH VANILLA SMOKED LABNE

500g (1lb) Greek yoghurt

¼ cup (55g) firmly packed brown sugar

1 vanilla pod, split lengthways, seeds scraped, pod reserved

50g (1½oz) smoking wood chips

10 fresh bay leaves

¾ cup (165g) caster (superfine) sugar

¼ cup (90g) honey

1 medium orange (240g), rind thinly peeled, then juiced

500g (1lb) plums, halved or quartered if large, stones removed

250g (8oz) blackberries

You will need to start this recipe 1 day ahead.

Combine yoghurt, brown sugar and vanilla seeds in a medium bowl; spoon mixture into a large sieve lined with muslin or a clean chux cloth set over a large bowl. Gather corners of cloth and twist; secure with kitchen string or an elastic band. Refrigerate overnight or until thickened. Untie cloth and pull back to expose labne.

Heat a covered gas barbecue with all burners set to low and hood closed.

Place smoking chips, bay leaves and reserved vanilla pod in a large flameproof saucepan. Increase burners to high. Place pan on grill. Using a blow torch, ignite chips and leaves until beginning to flame and smoke. Remove pan from heat. Place sieve over saucepan. Cover with foil. Stand for 30 minutes.

Meanwhile, combine caster sugar, honey, orange rind and juice, plums and blackberries in a flameproof roasting pan. Place in barbecue. Cook, with hood closed, stirring occasionally for 10 minutes or until fruit is tender. Remove; cool slightly.

Serve smoked labne topped with warm fruit. Drizzle with the fruit roasting juices.

TIPS Heating the chips over the stove while also igniting them with a blow torch ensures the chips continue to smoke, when they would otherwise go out. This technique is a great smoking hack and can also be done on a stovetop and oven.

SERVES 4

PREP + COOK TIME 35 MINUTES (+ REFRIGERATION)

SMOKED MILK PANNA COTTA WITH GRILLED PEACHES

35g (1oz) manuka wood chips, soaked

1½ cups (375ml) pouring cream

1½ cups (375ml) milk

¼ cup (55g) caster (superfine) sugar

4 tsp (13g) powdered gelatine

½ tsp orange blossom water

⅓ cup (75g) caster (superfine) sugar, extra

¼ cup (60ml) fig vino cotto

1 tbsp lemon juice

2 medium yellow peaches (300g), cut into 6 wedges each

micro herbs, to serve

Place wood chips in the centre of a large piece of foil; wrap tightly to enclose. Place parcel in the base of a large wok set over high heat (see tip). Set a round metal trivet or wok rack over parcel.

Place cream, milk and sugar in a 1 litre (4-cup) heatproof flan dish. When parcel begins to smoke, set flan dish on top of trivet. Cover with lid or foil (not too tightly as airflow is essential). Allow to smoke for 5 minutes, stirring cream mixture every minute to prevent a skin forming and to dissolve sugar. Remove from wok; transfer mixture to a large bowl.

Combine gelatine and 1½ tablespoons water in a small jug. Stand for 3 minutes to soften. Stir in ½ cup (125ml) of the warm smoked milk mixture until gelatine dissolves. Place bowl with remaining milk mixture over a large bowl filled with ice. Whisk combined gelatine mixture and orange blossom water into milk mixture until chilled. Pour mixture back into flan dish. Refrigerate for 3 hours or until set.

Meanwhile, heat a covered gas barbecue with flat plate, with all burners set to high and hood closed. (Alternatively, heat a large frying pan over high heat on the stove.)

Stir extra sugar and ⅓ cup (80ml) water in a medium saucepan over medium-high heat. Bring to a gentle simmer. Simmer for 4 minutes. Remove from heat. Stir in vino cotto and lemon juice.

Cook peaches on flat plate or in frying pan for 1 minute on each cut-side, or until golden and charred. Transfer to a tray and drizzle with vino cotto mixture; leave to cool.

To serve, invert panna cotta onto a serving platter. Top with drained peaches and scatter with micro herbs. Drizzle with extra vino cotto, if you like.

TIP You could use the barbecue wok burner to smoke the milk mixture, if preferred.

GLOSSARY

ALLSPICE also called pimento or Jamaican pepper; tastes like a combination of nutmeg, cumin, clove and cinnamon. Available whole or ground.

ANCHOVIES small oily fish. Anchovy fillets are preserved and packed in oil or salt in small cans or jars, and are strong in flavour. Fresh anchovies are much milder in flavour.

BAHARAT an aromatic spice blend, includes some or all of the following: mixed spice, black pepper, allspice, dried chilli flakes, paprika, coriander seeds, cinnamon, clove, sumac, nutmeg, cumin seeds and cardamom seeds. It is often sold as Lebanese seven-spice, and can be found in Middle-Eastern food stores and specialist food stores.

BAKING POWDER a raising agent consisting mainly of two parts cream of tartar to one part bicarbonate of soda (baking soda).

BERBERE SPICE MIX essential to East African cooking, berbere spice gives wats (stews) of meat, vegetables or lentils their signature flavour. A blend of chilli, cardamom, fenugreek and other spices, it is used in staples like doro wat (chicken stew) and misir wat (red lentil stew), and is commonly eaten with injera, a fermented flatbread.

BULGUR also called burghul wheat; hulled steamed wheat kernels that, once dried, are crushed into various sized grains. Is not the same as cracked wheat.

BUTTERMILK originally the term given to the slightly sour liquid left after butter was churned from cream, today it is made from no-fat or low-fat milk to which specific bacterial cultures have been added.

CELERIAC (CELERY ROOT) tuberous root with knobbly brown skin, white flesh and a celery-like flavour.

CHEESE

fetta Greek in origin; a crumbly goat- or sheep-milk cheese with a sharp, salty taste. Ripened and stored in salted whey.

haloumi a firm, cream-coloured sheep-milk cheese matured in brine; haloumi can be grilled or fried, briefly, without breaking down. Should be eaten while still warm as it becomes tough and rubbery on cooling.

mozzarella soft, spun-curd cheese; originating in southern Italy where it was traditionally made from water-buffalo milk. Has a low melting point and elasticity when heated.

parmesan also called parmigiano; is a hard, grainy cow-milk cheese originating in the Parma region of Italy. The curd for this cheese is salted in brine for a month, then aged for up to 2 years in humid conditions.

pecorino the Italian generic name for cheeses made from sheep milk. This family of hard, white to pale-yellow cheeses, have been matured for 8 to 12 months. If you can't find it, use parmesan instead.

ricotta a soft, sweet, moist, white cow-milk cheese with a low fat content and a slightly grainy texture. The name roughly translates as 'cooked again' and refers to ricotta's manufacture from a whey that is itself a by-product of cheese making.

CHORIZO sausage of Spanish origin, made of coarsely ground pork and highly seasoned with garlic and chilli. They are deeply smoked, very spicy and dry-cured, so don't require cooking.

CORIANDER (CILANTRO) a bright-green leafy herb with a pungent flavour. Both stems and roots of coriander are used in cooking; wash well before using. Also available ground or as seeds; these should not be substituted for fresh as the tastes are completely different.

CREAM

pouring also called pure or fresh cream; it contains no additives and a minimum fat content of 35%.

sour a thick commercially-cultured soured cream with a 35% fat content.

thick (double) dolloping cream with a minimum fat content of 45%.

thickened (heavy) a whipping cream that contains a thickener. It has a minimum fat content of 35%.

DAIKON also called white radish. The flesh is white but the skin can be either white or black; buy those that are firm and unwrinkled.

ESCHALOTS also called French shallots or goldenshallots. Small and elongated, with a brown-skin, they grow in tight clusters similar to garlic.

FLOUR, BREAD also called gluten-enriched, strong or bread-mix flour. Produced from a wheat variety which has a high gluten (protein) content and is best suited for pizza and bread making: the expansion caused by the yeast and the stretchiness imposed by kneading require a flour that is "strong" enough to handle these stresses.

GELATINE we use dried (powdered) gelatine in this book; it's also available in sheet form known as leaf gelatine. A thickening agent made from either collagen, or certain algae (agar-agar). Three teaspoons of dried gelatine (8g or one sachet) is about the same as 4 gelatine leaves.

GHEE clarified butter; with the milk solids removed, this fat has a high smoking point so can be heated to a high temperature without burning. Used as a cooking medium in most Indian recipes.

GRAPEVINE LEAVES from early spring, fresh grapevine leaves can be found in greengrocers. Alternatively, cryovac-packages containing about 60 leaves in brine can be found in Middle Eastern food shops and some delicatessens; these must be well rinsed and dried before using.

HARISSA a North African paste made from dried red chillies, garlic, olive oil and caraway seeds. It is available from Middle Eastern food shops and some supermarkets.

KECAP MANIS a thick soy sauce with added sugar and spices. The sweetness comes from the addition of molasses or palm sugar.

MIRIN a Japanese champagne-coloured cooking wine; made of glutinous rice and alcohol and used expressly for cooking.

ONION
green (scallions) also called, incorrectly, shallot; an immature onion picked before the bulb has formed. Has a long, bright-green edible stalk.
red also known as Spanish, red or Bermuda onion; a sweet-flavoured, purple-red onion.

PINE NUTS also known as pignoli; not in fact a nut but a small, cream-coloured kernel from pine cones. They are best roasted before use.

POMEGRANATE MOLASSES not to be confused with pomegranate syrup or grenadine; pomegranate molasses is thicker, browner and more concentrated in flavour.

SICHUAN PEPPERCORNS native to the Sichuan province of China. Although it is not related to the peppercorn family, small, red-brown aromatic Sichuan berries look like black peppercorns and have a distinctive peppery-lemon flavour and aroma.

TAMARIND PUREE the distillation of tamarind juice into a condensed, compacted form. Gives a sweet-sour, slightly astringent taste to sauces, marinades and dressings.

TURMERIC also called kamin; is a rhizome related to galangal and ginger. Must be grated or pounded to release its acrid aroma and pungent flavour. Known for the golden colour it imparts, fresh turmeric can be substituted with the more commonly found dried powder.

VINEGAR
apple cider made from fermented apples.
balsamic made from the juice of Trebbiano grapes; it is a deep rich brown colour with a sweet and sour flavour.
rice made from rice wine lees (sediment left after fermentation), salt and alcohol.
wine based on red wine.

WATERCRESS one of the cress family, a large group of peppery greens used raw in salads, dips and sandwiches, or cooked in soups. Highly perishable, so it must be used as soon as possible after purchase.

YEAST a raising agent used in dough making. Granular (7g sachets) and fresh compressed (20g blocks) yeast can usually be substituted for the other when yeast is called for.

ZA'ATAR a Middle Eastern herb and spice mixture which varies; always includes thyme, with ground sumac and, usually, toasted sesame seeds.

CONVERSION CHART

MEASURES

One Australian metric measuring cup holds approximately 250ml; one Australian metric tablespoon holds 20ml; one Australian metric teaspoon holds 5ml. The difference between one country's measuring cups and another's is within a two- or three-teaspoon variance and will not affect your cooking results. North America, New Zealand and the United Kingdom use a 15ml tablespoon. All cup and spoon measurements are level.

The most accurate way of measuring dry ingredients is to weigh them.

When measuring liquids, use a clear glass or plastic jug with the metric markings.

We use extra-large eggs with an average weight of 60g.

DRY MEASURES

metric	imperial
15g	½oz
30g	1oz
60g	2oz
90g	3oz
125g	4oz (¼lb)
155g	5oz
185g	6oz
220g	7oz
250g	8oz (½lb)
280g	9oz
315g	10oz
345g	11oz
375g	12oz (¾lb)
410g	13oz
440g	14oz
470g	15oz
500g	16oz (1lb)
750g	24oz (1½lb)
1kg	32oz (2lb)

LIQUID MEASURES

metric	imperial
30ml	1 fluid oz
60ml	2 fluid oz
100ml	3 fluid oz
125ml	4 fluid oz
150ml	5 fluid oz
190ml	6 fluid oz
250ml	8 fluid oz
300ml	10 fluid oz
500ml	16 fluid oz
600ml	20 fluid oz
1000ml (1 litre)	1¾ pints

LENGTH MEASURES

metric	imperial
3mm	⅛in
6mm	¼in
1cm	½in
2cm	¾in
2.5cm	1in
5cm	2in
6cm	2½in
8cm	3in
10cm	4in
13cm	5in
15cm	6in
18cm	7in
20cm	8in
22cm	9in
25cm	10in
28cm	11in
30cm	12in (1ft)

OVEN TEMPERATURES

The oven temperatures in this book are for conventional and fan-forced ovens.

	°C (Celsius)	°F (Fahrenheit)
Very slow	120	250
Slow	150	300
Moderately slow	160	325
Moderate	180	350
Moderately hot	200	400
Hot	220	425
Very hot	240	475

INDEX